C. S. Lewis's *Perelandra*

C. S. Lewis's *Perelandra*

Reshaping the Image of the Cosmos

Edited by

JUDITH WOLFE

and

BRENDAN WOLFE

THE KENT STATE UNIVERSITY PRESS

Kent, Ohio

© 2013 by The Kent State University Press
All rights reserved
Library of Congress Catalog Number 2012048921
ISBN 978-1-60635-183-3
Manufactured in the United States of America

A version of "*Perelandra* in Its Own Time: A Modern View of the Space Trilogy," by Sanford Schwartz, originally appeared as "Why Wells Is from Mars, Bergson from Venus: Mapping Evolution in the *Space Trilogy*" in *C. S. Lewis: Views from Wake Forest*, edited by Michael Travers (© Zossima Press, 2008).

A version of "Voyage to Venus: Lewis's Imaginative Path to *Perelandra*," by Michael Ward, was originally published as part of chapter 8 ("Venus") in *Planet Narnia: The Seven Heavens in the Imagination of C. S. Lewis*, by Michael Ward (2008), and appears here by permission of Oxford University Press, USA.

LIBRARY OF CONGRESS CATALOGING-IN-PUBLICATION DATA
C. S. Lewis's Perelandra : reshaping the image of the cosmos /
edited by Judith Wolfe and Brendan Wolfe.
pages cm
ISBN 978-1-60635-183-3 (hardcover) ∞
1. a Lewis, C. S. (Clive Staples), 1898–1963. Perelandra.
I. Wolfe, J. E. (Judith Elisabeth), 1979– editor of compilation.
II. Wolfe, B. N. (Brendan N.) editor of compilation.
PR6023.E926P4737 2013
823'912—dc23
2012048921

17 16 15 14 13   5 4 3 2 1

Contents

Free to Fall: The Moral Ground of Events on Perelandra

Introduction

The Scope and Vision of This Study

JUDITH WOLFE

Perelandra is unparalleled among C. S. Lewis's works in the audacity and grandeur of its conception. This collection of essays brings together a world-class group of literary, theological, and Lewisian scholars to examine the scope of this conception and work out some of its practical implications.

Lewis is a scholar whose originality is indivisible from his commitment to tradition, both Christian and literary; his work is the flower of an imagination inseminated by ancient truth. Of *Perelandra*, Lewis said that it had all begun with a "mental picture of the floating islands. The whole of the rest of my labours in a sense consisted of building up a world in which floating islands could exist."[1] What kind of world this would be was overdetermined from within a diverse range of sources: literary, religious, historical, and scientific. That it should be Venus was suggested by a curious convergence: the scientific belief, in Lewis's time, that the surface of the planet Venus was liquid, and the classical imagination of the goddess Venus as Aphrodite Anaduomenê, the goddess rising out of the sea. That this newborn world of Venusian beauty should be a version of the Judeo-Christian paradise was suggested by both literary and religious history. In literary terms, the bordered isles were natural versions of the enclosed pleasure gardens of Elizabethan life and literature, themselves conscious imitations of the *paradise*—literally "enclosed garden"—of Ancient Near Eastern myth. And this inescapably brought with it the religious idea of a new Eden—a world not (yet) fallen into sin. Once all these associations were given shape, "of course the story about an averted fall developed. This is because, as you know, having got your people to this exciting country, something must happen."[2]

This throwaway remark already suggests that the spiritual dimension of Lewis's book accrued to the cosmological one not in a forced or arbitrary way but naturally. In fact, Lewis thought that science fiction in general couldn't function without a spiritual dimension: "No merely physical strangeness or merely spatial distance will realize that idea of *otherness* which is what we are always trying to grasp in a story about voyaging through space: you must go into another dimension. To construct plausible and moving 'other worlds' you must draw on the only real 'other world' we know, that of spirit."[3]

In *Perelandra,* the two are indistinguishable. The Cambridge philologist Elwin Ransom is carried by angelic powers to Venus (or, in the Old Solar tongue, Perelandra), a young planet covered by a golden sea on the surface of which luxuriantly verdant floating islands glide in and out of touch, overlooked by only one mass of mountainous fixed land. A first man and a first woman, majestic but also childlike, spend their days moving freely from island to island—at once the "noble savages" of Romantic literature and the Adam and Eve of Milton's *Paradise Lost.* The convergence of primitive innocence and Edenic majesty is particularly clear in an early verse draft:

> The floating islands, the flat golden sky
> At noon, the peacock sunset: tepid waves
> With the land sliding over them like a skin:
> The alien Eve, green-bodied, stepping forth
> To meet my hero from her forest home,
> Proud, courteous, unafraid; no thought infirm
> Alters her cheek—[4]

Unbeknownst to Ransom, however, the astrophysicist Weston has also traveled to Perelandra, in the service of a vision of emergent evolution and space colonization. Allowing himself to be possessed by the blind Force that he believes moves the universe, Weston divests himself of his humanity and becomes a medium of evil, an evil with the monomaniacal aim of tempting the Lady into transgressing the one commandment of her Creator: never to sleep on the Fixed Land. Feeling frustrated and paralyzed by this onslaught, Ransom asks how God can allow this, only to realize that he himself has been sent to avert this second fall. First through argument and finally through physical battle, Ransom tries to overcome the tempter, whose death in the subterranean caverns of the Fixed Land releases the new humanity from temptation and ushers in the coronation of the Green Lady and her King as rulers of Perelandra, supplanting the tutelary deity of the sphere, Venus.

What is remarkable in this retelling of Genesis 2–3 is that the seminal image of Lewis's other world—the floating islands of Venus—does not give way (like an incidental backdrop) to the increasingly focal religious story of an averted fall but is allowed to inflect Lewis's entire rendering of that story. This commitment both to an originary image and to the disparate sets of traditions that accrue to it—modern and medieval cosmology, classical mythology, and Christianity—propels Lewis to rethink both the contents and the functions of all four traditions. Not content with their coexistence in his novel, he creates a framework for his story that synthesizes the traditions of cosmology, mythology, and Christianity, all the while subtly reimagining each. The first part of this book is concerned with that reconfiguration.

Walter Hooper sets the stage with an intimate and lively account of the genesis of the Ransom Trilogy. In "C. S. Lewis and the Anthropological Approach," he recounts his first discussions about *Perelandra* with Lewis, emphasizing Lewis's understanding of the way "sources" function in the book. Sources, insists Lewis, are a springboard for, not the defining parameter of, an author's imagination: To read *Perelandra* solely through the lens of one particular set of sources is to import (now outdated) anthropological methods into literary study, and to distort the object of enquiry from the start.

Michael Ward complements Hooper's biographical account with a conceptual one. In his programmatic essay, "Voyage to Venus: Lewis's Imaginative Path to Perelandra," Ward presents Lewis's thought about the planet Venus as it is developed in his academic work, his poetry, and even his apologetics, and discusses the influence of that oeuvre on the creation of *Perelandra*. Ward concludes that *Perelandra*, as a story about the planet of love, is best described by the term *plenitude.*

The idea of plenitude is not only imaginatively but also theologically important, for, theologically, Lewis's book presents our own modern view of the cosmos as merely a shadowy image of the Perelandran, distorted by the veil surrounding our own "silent planet." Lewis's description, elsewhere, of the difference between allegory and symbolism gives a clue to his aim here: "The allegorist leaves the given—his own passions—to talk of that which is confessedly less real. The symbolist leaves the given to find that which is more real. To put the difference in another way, for the symbolist, it is we who are the allegory."[5] In the cosmos as the eldila and Perelandrans behold it—a light-suffused "Deep Heaven"—we are meant to recognize the reality, of which our own image of the cosmos—*le silence éternel de ces espaces infinis qui nous effraie*—is only the dark underbelly.

This change of perspective is thoroughly theological. The profusion of light and life that characterizes Deep Heaven also characterizes the planet Perelandra; both reveal the natural conditions of life that, on Earth, have been curtailed by the besiegement of the "bent" eldil. Thus, the conditions of *scarcity* existing on Earth, which determine all relations to self and others there and that first make it attractive—indeed, almost needful—to steal for gain, lie for reputation, kill for safety, or covet for advantage, are exposed as unnatural deprivations resulting from the "Great Siege"—in Christian parlance, the Fall. On Perelandra, in contrast, scarcity gives way to a glorious plenitude of all good things, both tangible and spiritual. In the midst of this plenitude, there is no need to lie, steal, murder, or covet: All things are gift. The only way to sin is to refuse this gift in a perverse attempt to create one's own reality. (More about that later.)

Lewis's attempt to imaginatively restore the plenitude of "natural" human existence extends to an audacious attempt to unite "myth" and "fact" by integrating pagan mythology and the Christian story. He imagines a universe in which the pagan gods are real (and identified with "angels" or "Intelligences"—or, in the language of the novel, "eldila") and rule the planets that bear their names, but are subordinated to the new hierarchy established by the Incarnation. Into this universe, a new man and woman are created on Perelandra, and, like Adam and Eve, are tempted to fall. But because the Incarnation has already occurred on another planet, (Earthly) man is now not only a bearer of sin but also a potential mediator of salvation—and, indeed, the new Lady is both tempted and defended by humans who have made their way to Perelandra.

The entire cosmos, here, is a great dance, and God, unlike in Dante's vision, is not the still center of the dance of creation but the main dancer.

In his essay, Paul Fiddes offers a magisterial account of this culminating, mystical image of *Perelandra*—the Great Dance in which the entire cosmos joins or will join at the end of time. Setting it in the context of both the Neoplatonic tradition of the dance of the spheres and Lewis's own theological writings, Fiddes examines the significance of a vision in which the Trinity itself *is* the primal dance, and in which the very point of human life is that "the whole dance . . . of this three-Personal life is to be played out in each one of us: or (putting it the other way round) each one of us has got to . . . take his place in that dance."

Lewis's vision of a dance led, rather than merely watched, by God is both thoroughly Christian and a bold move beyond the Neoplatonic tradition historically dominating Christianity, in which stasis is the ideal and motion the deviation. This theological innovation is not only hinted at in the Great Dance but written into the very structure of the planet. Perelandra's surface is in perpetual motion; the only divine prohibition is to refuse ever-impending change by remaining on the fixed land. For Sanford Schwartz, this emphasis on Becoming over Being amounts to an "inversion of Platonism," best explored in its relation to the evolutionary thought of Lewis's time, epitomized by Henri Bergson (whom Lewis caricatures in Weston). For Schwartz, Lewis's world is a sublimated form of Weston's (or Bergson's) "creative" or "emergent" evolution, showing how the fertile but flawed reconception of time in creative evolution may be "raised up" onto a higher plane and synthesized with the traditional conception of a transcendent Creator in whose image we are made. In other words, just as Bergson and his successors transfigured a theory of evolution still entangled in the static categories of traditional metaphysics and mechanistic science into a new principle of dynamic development, so Lewis transfigures Bergson's creative evolution, reversing his naturalization of the supernatural and reshaping his model of cosmic progress into a Christian vision of Becoming.

This reimagination of the Christian cosmos, creatively transforming the classical and medieval models that have always informed Christian theology, extends to the hierarchy of genders. Monika Hilder, in "Surprised by the Feminine," argues that *Perelandra* reveals a deeper and liberating meaning of the traditional (and potentially oppressive) hierarchy of man and woman, namely the relationship of God and man. Asserting that "we are all feminine vis-à-vis God," she argues that it is in the acknowledgment of his existential subordination and responsiveness—in the virtues of submission, obedience, and humility—that Ransom can achieve his mission. In other words, Lewis develops here a "theological feminism" that subverts the classical model of masculine heroism by celebrating the so-called "feminine" nature of (all) spiritual power and so makes available the "gender metaphor" as a means of spiritual and psychological empowerment for all humans: "This mystery is great: but I speak in regard of Christ and of the church" (Eph. 5:32, American Standard Version).

If, as Hilder argues, *Perelandra* unfolds a deeper and liberating meaning of the traditional and potentially oppressive hierarchy of man and woman, then what Lewis does here is to take seriously his own dual contention in *The Discarded Image* that the medieval image of a hierarchical cosmos is both deeply appealing and emphatically an *image* that must not be reified. In his own fiction, he creatively engages that realization by transforming the physical model of the medieval cosmos into a moral metaphor. Just as Hilder shows this for Lewis's gender imagery, Nikolay Epplée shows it for the medieval model of the order of the spheres: a universe with the Earth at its center and the *primum mobile* at its rim. Drawing on a wealth of literary and theological sources, Epplée shows the confluence of cosmological and moral dimensions in this important medieval trope of center and rim. To the Satanic Un-man, life is only a thin rim of superficial (and deceptive) meaning concealing a vast core of nothingness, unpenetrated by God. To the Christian Ransom (as to the pilgrim Dante), the farthest Heaven turns out to be the very center of the universe, which suffuses all things with glory. But this inversion is primarily a moral one: to see the real center, you have to cease pretending to be the center yourself.

The second part of this book examines the relationship of morality and meaning that the first part has begun to establish. In so doing, it focuses in on the fact that *Perelandra* effects the shifts of perspective discussed above to a particular narrative and theological purpose: to show (not merely to tell) what prelapsarian innocence may have been like and to respond to the age-old question of how it might be possible for evil to enter a wholly good world. Lewis's world of Venusian plenty lavishly illustrates the Platonic–Augustinian understanding of evil as a deprivation of being: everything that is, insofar as it exists and is itself, is good. The only way the Tempter can introduce evil—that is, sin—into such a world is to turn its lady away from the reality of her life and the world as gifts, and of herself as gifted. The result is a peculiar and fascinating depiction of temptation inflected by Lewis's central image of a floating world. The *faculty* to which Weston appeals is the imagination, and the *content* of his temptation is a rejection of the beneficent change written into the topography and governance of the planet in favor of imaginatively clinging to an earlier, expected, or imagined reality.

The essays in the second part of the book illuminate different aspects and implications of this dynamic. Meriel Patrick and Tami van Opstal analyze the structure of (religious) truth and knowledge on Perelandra, and relate it to the question of human freedom. Opstal discusses the Perelandran confluence of myth and fact by reference to Owen Barfield's theory of the development of consciousness, which claims that myths and metaphors are the last vestiges of a primordial state of consciousness that recognized the fundamental unity of physical and spiritual realities. She argues that the Green Lady is still in this state of "original participation," and that the novel is, in part, a story about the rupture of this participation and the possibility of evolving, or returning, toward "final participation."

Although Opstal focuses on the similarities between Lewis and Barfield, it is important to note that *Perelandra* is also a reiteration and illustration of the position Lewis defended in his 1925–27 "Great War" with Barfield. While Barfield, a budding anthroposophist, maintained that the deepest truths were incomprehensible to reason and accessible only to the greater faculty of the imagination, Lewis argued that the imagination was not a truth-telling faculty but neutral with regard to truth value, and that its apprehensions must always be checked against other sources of truth, including reason and authority. In *Perelandra,* he goes farther in his opposition to Barfield: In a world like Perelandra, in which truth is not (as in our world) obscured by deficient or distorted knowledge, temptation toward evil can proceed only via the imagination. Because it is capable of creating a world "alongside" the real world, the imagination inherently tends toward that "deprivation of being" that characterizes evil. Here Lewis, at his most radical, is affirming the principle stated by Aslan to Lucy in *The Voyage of the Dawn Treader:* "Child," said Aslan, "did I not explain to you once before that no one is ever told what would have happened?"

This very negative evaluation of the imagination raises the question of the relationship between the Lady's constitution and that of the reader, who lives in a world in which (religious) knowledge *is* obscured. It is this question that engages Meriel Patrick in her essay, "Myth, Pluralism, and Choice: *Perelandra* and Lewis on Religious Truth." Patrick argues that the Perelandrans confront no serious choices regarding religious belief: they enjoy an intimate relationship with God and certainty of the truths he reveals. For most readers, on the other hand, questions of whether God exists at all and whether any seeming communication from Him is authentic, are inalienable and even central aspects of the experience of religious faith. Patrick discusses this discrepancy with relation to the question of human freedom and elaborates the response Lewis offers in his novel.

But there is another aspect to the question of how the negative role of the imagination on Perelandra relates to our own experience—namely, how to reconcile Lewis's theological assessment of the imagination in *Perelandra* with the form of the novel itself, which is as imaginative as any he produced. Bruce Johnson gives a partial response to this question by relating the moral experience of the characters to the form of the novel. In "Frightful Freedom: *Perelandra* as Imaginative Theodicy," he argues that Ransom discovers that rational arguments alone are insufficient weapons to fully counter the embodiment of evil present in the Un-man, and he learns that he must move from theory to practice, becoming an active participant siding with God and against evil. In following Ransom's path, the reader vicariously experiences the same emotional, volitional, and mystical resolutions of the problem of evil as Ransom, exploring various ways to ultimately resolve evils that defy rational explanations. In this context, the closing scenes on Perelandra may best be judged not as didactic but as an attempt to draw the reader into a mystical experience. Neither emotion nor intellect can fully contain the mystery, and Lewis leaves the reader with unanswered longing that can only be engaged in the reader's own life.

The last essay in the collection confronts head-on the question, lurking in the background of much of part 2, of the relationship between innocence and free will. In a letter of May 8, 1954, Lewis states that free will or choice is a necessary condition of the Fall. He states further that such choice renders the Fall avoidable. Taking his cue from the letter, Michael Travers studies the matter of free will in the events on Perelandra, asking specifically whether or not a fall into sin is a legitimate possible outcome for Tinidril. One of Lewis's basic assumptions in *Perelandra* is that unfallenness (innocence) and free will are by no means incompatible; on the contrary, free will makes a moral fall possible. The depiction of an unfallen character therefore does not abrogate the potential for moral conflict, but rather displays it in paradigmatic form. Conversely, it offers a new perspective on free will that challenges the usual modern understanding of free will as existing only within a tendency toward evil.

Together, these essays lead the reader further into Lewis's novel, not only showing the scope of his intellectual and imaginative work but also pursuing the urgent questions arising from that reimagination of the cosmos.

NOTES

1. C. S. Lewis, "Unreal Estates," in his *EC* I (London: HarperCollins, 2000), 122.

2. Ibid.

3. C. S. Lewis, "On Stories," in his *EC* I, 90 (emphasis added). The reverse also held true for Lewis: The sense of "otherness" that science fiction sometimes evokes so successfully through the image of outer space or a parallel world does not actually have to do with any *place* at all, but with the undeniable presence of "spirit" in a physical universe. "No man would find an abiding strangeness on the Moon unless he were the sort of man who could find it in his own back garden" ("On Stories," *EC* I, 90).

4. An early verse fragment of *Perelandra*, quoted in Walter Hooper's *C. S. Lewis: A Companion and Guide* (London: HarperCollins, 1996), 220; the form was abandoned immediately afterward in favor of prose.

5. C. S. Lewis, *AOL* (Oxford: Oxford Univ. Press, 1970), 45.

Abbreviations for Works by C. S. Lewis

Throughout, Lewis's own full-length works are referred to by the following abbreviations, here listed with their original dates of publication. Parenthetical text citations are only to Lewis's works. The facts of publication for specific editions of his works cited in the individual essays in this book are given at first mention in the endnotes for each chapter.

AGO	*A Grief Observed.* By N. W. Clerk (pseud.). 1961.
AMR	*All My Road Before Me: The Diary of C. S. Lewis, 1922–1927.* Edited by Walter Hooper. 1991.
AOL	*The Allegory of Love: A Study in Medieval Tradition.* London: Clarendon Press, 1936.
CL I	*The Collected Letters of C. S. Lewis.* Vol. 1: *Family Letters 1905–1931.* Edited by Walter Hooper. 2000.
CL II	*The Collected Letters of C. S. Lewis.* Vol. 2: *Books, Broadcasts, and the War, 1931–1949.* Edited by Walter Hooper. 2004.
CL III	*The Collected Letters of C. S. Lewis.* Vol. 3: *Narnia, Cambridge, and Joy, 1950–1963.* Edited by Walter Hooper. 2006.
CP	*The Collected Poems of C. S. Lewis.* Edited by Walter Hooper. 1994.
CR	*Christian Reflections.* Edited by Walter Hooper. 1967.
DI	*The Discarded Image: An Introduction to Medieval and Renaissance Literature.* 1964.
EC I	*Essay Collection: Literature, Philosophy and Short Stories.* Edited by Lesley Walmsley. 2000.
EC II	*Essay Collection: Faith, Christianity, and the Church.* Edited by Lesley Walmsley. 2000.
EIC	*An Experiment in Criticism.* 1961.
EL	*English Literature in the Sixteenth Century, Excluding Drama.* Oxford History of English literature; Clark lectures. 1954.

FL   *The Four Loves.* 1960.

GD   *God in the Dock: Essays on Theology and Ethics.* Edited by Walter Hooper. 1970.

LB   *The Last Battle: A Story for Children.* 1956.

LTM   *Prayer: Letters to Malcolm.* 1964.

LWW   *The Lion, the Witch, and the Wardrobe: A Story for Children.* 1950.

M   *Miracles: A Preliminary Study.* 1947.

MC   *Mere Christianity.* 1952.

NP   *Narrative Poems.* Edited by Walter Hooper. 1969.

OSP   *Out of the Silent Planet.* 1938.

OTOW   *Of This and Other Worlds.* Edited by Walter Hooper. 1982.

P   *Perelandra: A Novel.* 1943.

PP   *The Problem of Pain.* 1940.

PPL   *A Preface to Paradise Lost, Being the Ballard Matthews Lectures, Delivered at University College, North Wales, 1941.* 1942.

PR   *The Pilgrim's Regress: An Allegorical Apology for Christianity, Reason and Romanticism.* 1933.

RP   *Reflections on the Psalms.* 1958.

SBJ   *Surprised by Joy: The Shape of My Early Life.* 1955.

SIL   *Spenser's Images of Life.* Edited by Alastair Fowler. 1967.

SIW   *Studies in Words.* 1960.

SL   *The Screwtape Letters.* 1942.

SLE   *Selected Literary Essays.* Edited by Walter Hooper. 1969.

SMRL   *Studies in Medieval and Renaissance Literature.* Edited by Walter Hooper. 1966.

TGD   *The Great Divorce.* 1945.

THS   *That Hideous Strength: A Modern Fairy-tale for Grown-ups.* 1945.

TWHF   *Till We Have Faces: A Myth Retold.* 1956.

U   *Undeceptions: Essays on Theology and Ethics.* Edited by Walter Hooper. 1971.

WG   *The Weight of Glory and Other Addresses.* 1949.

C. S. Lewis and the
Anthropological Approach

WALTER HOOPER

I was one of that generation of Americans who discovered C. S. Lewis just as he was beginning to be well known in the States. That was fifty years ago, and, like many others, I remain indebted to Chad Walsh and his first book about Lewis—*C. S. Lewis: Apostle to the Skeptics* (1949). It's still my favorite book on Lewis, and though many of today's readers know a hundred times more about Lewis than Walsh could have known when he wrote that work in 1949, Walsh knew how to illuminate the rare brilliance he found in Lewis's writings. When he pointed, it was usually to something one would not have seen on one's own. I have since come to see that what I like about Chad Walsh and appreciate most in other Lewis critics is not observations novel or inimical to Lewis, but those that help me appreciate what is already there.

While I never imagined I could emulate Chad Walsh, my chance to write something useful about Lewis came in 1962 when, as a young instructor in English at the University of Kentucky, I was awarded the contract to write a volume on C. S. Lewis for the Twayne's English Author Series. I had been corresponding off and on with Lewis since 1954. Now, on being awarded that contract, I wrote to ask if he would see me if I went to Oxford. He said that he would be happy to meet me, but he went on to say, "I feel strongly that a man is ill advised to write a book on any living author. . . . Far better write about the unanswering dead!"[1]

But, of course, it was not really help with the book that I most wanted. Almost since I first came across his writings in 1953 I had longed to see

Lewis. Now it seemed I might not only see him but meet him as well. When I arrived in Oxford in June 1963, I had already written several chapters of the Twayne book, all ready to show Lewis. I must note that I was under no illusion that I was likely to meet Lewis more than once. In fact, I had got it into my head that a single meeting would be it.

I have so often described my first meeting with Lewis, which occurred on June 7, 1963, that I dare not inflict my readers with it again. What I will say of that first meeting, however, was that the moment I met Lewis I forgot my book. If I had thought of it, I think I would have sat on it or thrown it out the window, for I felt something of that certainty of Orual who said, when confronted with the object of her desire, "I know now, Lord, why you utter no answer. You are yourself the answer."[2] By this I mean that, much as I admired everything Lewis wrote, he was more than his books.

But lest I make Lewis sound less than real, let me mention something that made him seem very solid indeed. I presented Lewis with a souvenir of my little home town in North Carolina—a case of cigarettes with filter tips. "Thanks very much," he said, "I'll give them to my house-keeper. My brother and I don't smoke cigarettes with contraceptives on the end."

We turned from the cigarettes with contraceptives to other more interesting topics, one of which was Lewis's interplanetary novels. I asked which of his books he thought best and he named *Perelandra.* He then asked in return, "Which do you like the most?"

"I agree with you—*Perelandra* is the best," I replied.

"But notice," said Lewis, "I didn't ask which you thought *best,* but which you *liked* the most."

"Oh, in that case," I said, "I like *That Hideous Strength* more than any of your works."

"So do I," said Lewis, "but don't you see that there is a difference between what you think best and what you like most?" This is a very important distinction.

This meeting, of about two hours, ended with Lewis walking me to the bus stop. Thinking that we had just had our one and only meeting, I was thanking him when he said, "You're not getting away!" and invited me to a meeting of the Inklings the following Monday.

There were eight of us at that meeting in the Lamb and Flag, and another visitor attended besides me—Roger Lancelyn Green, a semiregular member of the Inklings. He was a man whose books I admired very much, and Lewis saw to it that we spent a good deal of time discussing Green's *King Arthur and the Knights of the Round Table* (1953), in which he makes a particular feature of Logres, the hidden Arthurian kingdom within Britain. Writing about that meeting in his diary, Roger noted that one of those in the Lamb and Flag that day was Walter Hooper, "who is writing some sort of book or thesis about Jack."[3] I had mentioned my Twayne book to Roger when he asked me what I was doing in Oxford. The one to whom I could not bring myself to mention it was Lewis.

This was because the book paled into insignificance beside his talk and the man himself. More than anything, I wanted to drink in everything he was saying. Lewis by no means did all the talking, or even much of it. But he made good talk possible, and he brought out of others the best they had. I remember thinking how unusually sensible my own conversation had suddenly become. Although the others knew Lewis well, I have since come to believe that one of the things we all found attractive about Lewis was something he liked about his tutor at Great Bookham, Mr Kirkpatrick—the "Great Knock." Lewis's conversation was "red beef and strong beer." We could say of Lewis, as he did of Kirkpatrick, "Here was talk that was really about something. Here was a man who thought not about you but about what you said."[4]

Then something happened that caused me to fear I was out of my depth. As we walked out of the pub at the meeting's end, Colin Hardie, one of the Inklings and the public orator for the University of Oxford, said: "How does Jack do it? His conversation makes me feel the top of my head is coming off!" If that distinguished man was so overwhelmed by Lewis's talk, what would happen to me? But Lewis knew how to temper the wind to the shorn lamb. As I walked away from the pub with Lewis, we paused so he could give some money to a beggar. I'm afraid I said the standard thing: "Aren't you afraid he'll spend it on drink?" To which Lewis said, "Well, if I kept it, *I* would!" Thinking the gathering in the Lamb and Flag must be my final meeting with Lewis, I was very pleased when he told me to appear at the Kilns on Wednesday morning.

I was in for a pleasant surprise. Lewis had told me that his brother Warnie was in Ireland, and that Wednesday morning we sat in Warnie's study—a rare privilege, because this room was filled with the furniture from their childhood home in Belfast, Little Lea. Lewis was sitting at what had been their father's desk, where he had been writing, and I sat facing him. I had earlier asked what he did with his manuscripts and he told me that after writing a book, such as *The Lion, the Witch, and the Wardrobe,* he would turn the manuscript over and write another book on the other side. Once the pages were fully used, he would throw the manuscript away. I think he must have seen the horror on my face because he suddenly picked up a page on which he'd been writing and asked, "Would you like to have that?" Of course I said yes, and I think that this was the beginning of Lewis's warming to the idea that, to some of us, his manuscripts were precious. As time went on he was to put into my hands several of his manuscripts. We talked of many things that morning, but still I could not bring up my book.

After this, we met three times a week, Mondays at the Lamb and Flag, Wednesdays at the Kilns, and Sundays, when I accompanied Lewis to his parish church for the Eucharist and then returned with him to the Kilns for breakfast. As I have had occasion to mention, I found Lewis in a bad state when I went out to see him on Sunday, July 14. He was suffering from a combination of things, and he was going the next morning to the Acland Nursing Home for a blood transfusion. He explained that he needed help with his correspondence—at that moment his desk was covered with letters he didn't have the strength to answer—and he asked if I'd stop in Oxford and become his private secretary. I was enormously gratified, and said I would, so long as I could go back to the States and teach one final term.

Lewis was to be in hospital for two weeks, during which time we stayed busy with his correspondence. At his suggestion, I moved into the Kilns on July 26, before he came home on August 6. The next weeks were perhaps some of the happiest of my life, for while I never enjoyed anyone's company as much as Lewis's, I was no longer afraid of him, and he treated me as if I belonged there.

It was during this happy period that the subject of my Twayne's English Author book came up, raised not by me but by Lewis. "Isn't it about time," he said one evening, "we looked at the book you are writing about me?" And so I took out my chapter on the space trilogy, and, while he sat silent, puffing his pipe, I began reading aloud. To understand what followed, though, I must mention Lewis's essay "The Anthropological Approach," which he wrote for the Festschrift commemorating Tolkien's seventieth birthday in 1962.

The essay begins: "It is not to be disputed that literary texts can sometimes be of great use to the anthropologist. It does not immediately follow from this that anthropological study can make in return any valuable contribution to literary criticism."[5]

Lewis illustrates this with an example from the Arthurian scholar R. S. Loomis, who complained about the "astonishing disharmony" and "absurdities" in the literature of the Holy Grail. What Loomis was doing, Lewis explained, was "leaving the literary quality of these romances severely alone and [becoming] . . . exclusively interested in the pagan myths from which he believes them to be derived."[6] Thus, instead of thinking what the Grail is in, for instance, Chrétien de Troyes' *Conte du Graal*, or Malory's *Morte D'Arthur*, or Tennyson's *Idylls of the King*, Loomis judged those stories by the findings of Celtic scholars who maintain that objects such as cauldrons, knives, and horns found in Celtic romances are early instances of the same sacred objects that appear in the Grail legends. Lewis made the point with particular force in his essay "The Genesis of a Medieval Book":

> The text before us, however it came into existence, must be allowed to work on us in its *own* way, and must be judged on its *own* merits. . . . And while we are reading or criticizing we must be on our guard against a certain elliptical mode of expression which may be legitimate for some other purpose but is deadly for us. We must not say that the Grail "is" a Celtic cauldron of plenty, or that Malory's Gawain "is" a solar deity, or that the land of Gome in Chrétien's *Launcelot* "is" the world of the dead. Within a given story any object, person, or place is neither more nor less nor other than what that story effectively shows it to be. The ingredients of one story cannot be anything in another story, for they are not in it at all.[7]

At the end of "The Anthropological Approach," Lewis says, "Until our own age readers accepted this world as the romancers' 'noble and joyous' invention . . . There has now arisen a type of reader who cannot thus accept it. The tale in itself does not seem to him to provide adequate grounds for the feelings to which he is dimly aware that he is being prompted. He therefore invents new grounds for them in his own life as a reader. And he does this by building up round himself a second romance which he mistakes for reality."[8]

By this time, some of my readers might be eager to hear what I read aloud to C. S. Lewis, but while I know those chapters are somewhere among my papers, I cannot find them. Indeed, I have searched high and low because

I was keen to lay bare my embarrassment. (Imagine the worst thing you have ever written, then picture yourself reading it aloud to C. S. Lewis!)

As I remember, I was not so much writing a book as assembling a collection of pieces by other people who felt no qualms about explaining where Lewis got every idea in his interplanetary novels. This was a time when scholars talked mainly of "influences," and I believe that if one went back to the bibliography I'd compiled and read all those articles one would conclude that Lewis had created *Perelandra* and his other novels from other people's writings. I was, thus, a long way from the truism stated in "The Genesis of a Medieval Book" that "the ingredients of one story cannot be anything in another story, for they are not in it at all."

I can recall only two of the "influences" I discussed in the chapter on the cosmic trilogy that I read aloud to Lewis. The first was the author of an article I quoted who insisted that Lewis took his description of the Un-man's fingers as he slit open the bodies of the frogs directly from the description of Grendel's fingers in *Beowulf*. "Anthropological approach!" Lewis commented cheerfully. "I never thought of it." While that piece of "influence" may have been a stretch, I remember coming up with one that I knew *had* to have a bearing on *That Hideous Strength*. Someone had pointed out that the Head of Alcasan and the whole business of reducing Mankind to one or two heads, had to have derived from Edgar Rice Burroughs's *The Chessmen of Mars* (1922). In that story, Burroughs created on Mars an intelligent race whose individual members each took the form of a head with a powerful brain that was able to move with the aid of tiny, detachable legs.

I was sure I had backed Lewis into a corner with this one, but, smiling broadly, he boomed out, "Anthropological approach!!" adding, "I have never even heard of that story."

The only other point I can recall making in the passage I read to Lewis was that since Satan, as the Un-man, had not completely taken over Dr. Weston when Ransom killed him, this made Ransom a murderer.

"Anthropological approach!" yelled Lewis again. But in this case he made an interesting admission. "I never decided whether Weston was dead or not," he said. "I didn't think I had to decide, and I preferred to leave it undecided, on the fringe of the story." He went on to say that he did this consciously, not only in the interplanetary stories but also in the chronicles of Narnia. Where it was not necessary to decide what happened to some characters and some situations, he preferred to limit his knowledge as author.

By the time we got to the end of my absurd chapter on the interplanetary novels, Lewis had said "anthropological approach" of every one of my "influences." Perhaps if this had happened earlier in my friendship with Lewis I would have been humiliated, but by this time, I was as firmly convinced of the fallacy of the anthropological approach as he was. After all, I had experienced his titanic imagination for several months, not only in stories but in the brilliant light he continues to shine on our ancient faith. In the terms of Lewis's *Experiment in Criticism,* I realized that I had been "using" *Perelandra* and the other novels, rather than "receiving" from them.[9]

We discussed the anthropological approach and its relation to the interplanetary novels in several conversations during Lewis's convalescence. I was so annoyed with my own use of "influences" and "parallels" that I suggested that, if Lewis *had* to get an idea from Edgar Rice Burroughs, who must have, in turn, received it from someone else, who *had* to get it from someone else—then, logically, didn't every idea go back to Adam?

Lewis did not accept this, suggesting instead that ideas were being found and lost and found again. He had expressed this idea in an early letter to Arthur Greeves. "Don't you get the feeling," he asked Arthur, "of something waiting there and slowly being recovered in fragments by different human minds according to their abilities, and partially spoiled in each writer by the admixture of his own mere individual invention?"[10] Besides this, Lewis was quick to praise those authors who made a better use of something found in other writers, as, for instance, in his essay, "What Chaucer Really Did to *Il Filostrato.*" But the difference between what he did and what I attempted to do in my early exercise in criticism was very great. In his essay, he illuminated both Chaucer's *Troilus and Criseyde* and the work on which it is based, Boccaccio's *Il Filostrato.*

Let me mention another point about his borrowing. When I asked Lewis how he came to make the Lady and the King of Perelandra green, he said the idea came from Richard Burton's *Anatomy of Melancholy* (1621) where, writing about the inhabitants of other planets, Burton mentions "those two green children which Nubrigensis speaks of in his time, that fell from heaven."[11] I have yet to see how this piece of knowledge helps us to understand *Perelandra* better—except to show what a fine thing Lewis could bring out of very little.

In any event, the best thing to come out of what we might call my tutorial with Lewis over the anthropological approach was that it sent me back to the interplanetary stories and *Perelandra* with a new hunger. First of all, what had always impressed me was one of the things which set them apart perhaps from all other science fiction—the fact that the inhabitants of his other worlds are unfallen. "I think I have rather pulled the rug out from under the Establishment," said Lewis. This led us to discuss why more authors did not try the same thing. Lewis, as I remember, did not blame modern writers for not attempting this, because, as he said, Newman had found it "a contradiction in terms to attempt a sinless Literature of sinful man."[12] "One can only do one's best," said Lewis.

And what a wonderful "best" that turned out to be. If one reads *Perelandra* alongside Lewis's *Preface to Paradise Lost*, I don't think one finds a single shortcoming in Milton's poem that is not put right in what Lewis thought his best work.

But what, someone might ask, about my Twayne's English Author book? I might, perhaps, have tried rewriting it, but the direction of my life was changed when Lewis died and his brother, Warnie, invited me to edit Jack Lewis's literary remains. To make his unpublished writings available seemed infinitely more important than anything I could write, and I abandoned the Twayne project.

I did not, however, abandon the writings on Lewis of Chad Walsh and so many other fine critics and commentators. If the privilege of knowing C. S. Lewis for a short while taught me anything, it was, as he said in *An Experiment in Criticism*, that "the man who is contented to be only himself, and therefore less a person, is in prison. My own eyes are not enough for me; I will see through those of others" (*EIC*, 140). I'm sure I am only one of many who have understood or will understand *Perelandra* more fully for seeing it through the eyes of other thoughtful readers.

This group includes not only those who have written the essays in this volume but many who never commit their appreciation of Lewis to paper. I expect most of our appreciation derives from those who become our friends because, as Lewis said, "we see the same truth."[13] Do you recall Lewis's account of his first meeting with Arthur Greeves? The young Jack Lewis had gone to visit Arthur expecting nothing. But then he saw one of his favorite books on the table. "'Do *you* like that?' said I. 'Do *you* like that?' said he."

"Nothing, I suspect," Lewis went on to say, "is more astonishing in any man's life than the discovery that there do exist people very, very like himself" (*SBJ*, 125–26).

Not, of course, that you and I don't sometimes meet a critic who needs to be cured of my old fault—the anthropological approach.

Notes

1. C. S. Lewis to Walter Hooper, in Lewis, *CL* III (London: HarperCollins, 2007), 1355.

2. C. S. Lewis, *TWF* (London: Geoffrey Bles, 1956), 319.

3. Roger Lancelyn Green and Walter Hooper, *C. S. Lewis: A Biography* (London: Collins, 1974; rev. ed., 2002), 178.

4. C. S. Lewis, *SBJ* (London, Geoffrey Bles, 1955), 131.

5. C. S. Lewis, "The Anthropological Approach," in *SLE* (Cambridge, UK: Cambridge Univ. Press, 1969), 301.

6. Ibid., 302.

7. C. S. Lewis, "The Genesis of a Medieval Book," in *SMRL* (Cambridge, UK: Cambridge Univ. Press, 1966), 39–40.

8. Lewis, "Anthropological Approach," 310.

9. C. S. Lewis, *EIC* (Cambridge, UK: Cambridge Univ. Press, 1961), 19.

10. C. S. Lewis to Arthur Greeves, in *CL* I (London: HarperCollins, 2000), 935.

11. Richard Burton, *The Anatomy of Melancholy* (Oxford: J. Lichfield & J. Short for H. Cripps, 1621), pt. 2, sect. 2, mem. 3.

12. John Henry Newman, *The Idea of a University* (1852) Discourse 9, sect. 7.

13. C. S. Lewis, *FL* (London: Geoffrey Bles, 1960), 78.

The
Perelandran Cosmos

Voyage to Venus

Lewis's Imaginative Path to Perelandra

MICHAEL WARD

When I think of *Perelandra,* the word that comes immediately to mind is *plenitude.* Plenitude . . . abundance . . . bounty: these are the qualities that linger upon the imaginative palate. In this second volume of his Cosmic Trilogy,[1] Lewis has created a veritable cornucopia, almost overwhelming in the intensity and vitality of the sensory pleasures that it describes, heaping them lavishly, like the Danaëan shower of gold,[2] upon its fortunate hero, Ransom, and through him upon us readers also.

And if *plenitude* aptly describes Ransom's experience on Perelandra, and our experience in reading *Perelandra,* it is no less apt a term when it comes to surveying the novel from a critical and analytical standpoint, as this present volume does. What I mean by *plenitude* is perhaps usefully expressed by drawing a parallel with the twelve great feasts of the liturgical calendar of the Eastern Orthodox Church. These twelve great feasts, surprisingly, do not include the Feast of the Resurrection. That is because the Resurrection is a feast unto itself, the Feast of Feasts, in its own separate class, the completion and consummation of the other twelve. Plenitude, I suggest, should be regarded in a similar fashion vis-à-vis *Perelandra:* it should be seen as the quality that informs, envelops, and fulfils all the other literary, philosophical, and theological elements in the novel, not merely making of them a series of discrete banquets, pleasing to the intellect and the imagination in recognizable ways, but elevating them into a banquet of another order, a higher, epiphenomenal order, a whole new genus of literary pleasure.

Plenitude, plenty, plenteousness: the Perelandran Feast of Feasts. To other readers who may disagree that this is the essential flavor of the book, and who may wish to argue that their own favored aspect is the real center, I would reply, "Each is equally at the center and none are there by being equals, but some by giving place and some by receiving it, the small things by their smallness and the great by their greatness, and all the patterns linked and looped together by the unions of a kneeling with a sceptered love. Blessed be He!"[3] In other words, whichever feature of the pattern one's eye fixes upon becomes the center of the Great Dance and, also, the center of the book, and this is what I mean by plenitude: not just one particular aspect of the dance, but that very characteristic of the dance itself, its capacity to be more than the sum of its parts. All is central because all is loved. Perelandra is Venus, the planet of love, and love bears all things, believes all things, hopes all things, endures all things. All things come equally within the loving embrace of Venus; she will have no favorites among her children. She will not prefer the wave that has just gone to the wave that is about to come. She will not choose one fish to ride on more often than another. Every single thing in her domain will be enjoyed freely and with a perfect equilibrium of attention, both to its peculiar qualities and to its universal qualities. She will have no favorites because *all* are favorites.

When one's subject is plenitude, it is easy to lapse into thinking that plenitude is a "come-one-come-all" kind of multifariousness, an undiscriminating, bran-tub mentality. In fact, plenitude as Lewis presents it for our enjoyment in *Perelandra* is much more than just a bland "everything-ism." There is a peculiar identity to plenitude that distinguishes it from other things, and that quality comes, I would suggest, from Lewis's enduring, imaginative, and scholarly meditations upon the imagery associated with Venus.

In the rest of this essay, therefore, I wish to survey how Lewis gradually became more enamored of, and learned in, the personality of Venus during the years prior to his writing of *Perelandra*. Occasionally, where examples are particularly striking, I will glance forward to his continuing interest in Venus even after the writing of *Perelandra,* in order to emphasize just how long-lived and deep was his involvement with Venereal imagery. In so doing, I hope to provide a secure sense of Lewis's imaginative voyage to Venus and show how he arrived at the presentation of plenitude that is the center of the trilogy's central story.

Imaginative Preparation for *Perelandra*

"'Sweeter than all it is when one bed holds twain that love, and the queen of Cypris is praised of both.' Queen of Cypris, you know, is Aphrodite." Thus Lewis wrote to his friend Arthur Greeves, in 1917, quoting Asclepiades;[4] it is the first manifestation of his literary interest in the goddess of the third heaven. A year later, he recalls to Greeves's mind "the night when we first broached the 'nameless secrets of Aphrodite.'"[5] These nameless secrets, otherwise embarrassing or shameful to the young Lewis, became thinkable and discussible under the rubric of Aphrodite/Venus and the imagery associated with her, and it was around this time that he began to develop his abiding absorption in her qualities.

One area of interest encompassed musical expressions of her nature. Lewis listened to Wagner's *Tannhauser,* or as he called it, Wagner's "Venusburg music"; he listened to the "Bright Star of Eve" by Charles Gounod; he enjoyed Holst's "Planets Suite," with its interpretation of Venus as the bringer of peace.[6] Music, as we will see below, became an important component of his eventual Perelandran sub-creation.

In the visual arts, too, Lewis found valuable expressions of Venus's personality. While an undergraduate at Oxford, he hung a picture of Venus in his college rooms at University College, the picture in question probably being "The Mirror of Venus," though whether it was the painting of that name by Velasquez or Titian or Burne-Jones or some other artist is unclear.[7] Derek Brewer recalls that Bronzino's "Allegory of Venus and Cupid" used to hang in Lewis's rooms at Magdalen.[8] Alastair Fowler remembers also seeing there a "large, dim reproduction of Botticelli's 'Mars and Venus,'"[9] a painting that Lewis particularly valued. George Watson recalls how Lewis said that he liked to peruse it when he was in a "Warburgian state of mind."[10] It is a painting to which we will have cause to return at the end of this essay.

In addition to finding Venus a useful symbolic way of talking about love and sex, and in addition to learning how Venus had been treated over the centuries by composers and painters, Lewis began to write his own poems about her. "I have nearly finished the Venus poem and am full of ideas for another," he wrote to Greeves in 1919, and he mentioned further work on Venus-focused poetry in a letter to Leo Baker in 1921.[11] He also looked at Venus in the night sky, repeatedly mentioning his observations to his correspondents. To his brother in 1940, for instance, he wrote, "Every night Venus grows more spectacular. It is true *Chaucerian* weather!"[12] This mention of Geoffrey Chaucer takes us to an additional and even more extensive outlet for Lewis's developing interest in Venus: namely, his scholarship.

As a medieval scholar, Lewis was of course intimately acquainted with the works of Chaucer, and his seven-volume edition of Chaucer's complete works contains numerous marginal comments, underlinings, markings, and other annotations in his own hand that make for fascinating reading.[13] In the endleaves of volume 5, for instance, Lewis made an index of eight items that especially interested him: three of these eight are connected with Venus. In one, he notes Chaucer's description of Venus in "The Knight's Tale," which runs as follows:

> The statue of Venus, glorious for to se,
> Was naked, fletynge in the large see,
> And fro the navele doun al covered was
> With wawes grene, and brighte as any glas.
> A citole in hir right hand hadde she,
> And on hir heed, ful semely for to se,
> A rose garland, fressh and wel smellynge;
> Above hir heed hir dowves flikerynge. (lines 1955ff)

Lewis glosses *citole* as "a stringed instrument," and although, when he came to create his own Green Lady on Perelandra, he does not have her playing an instrument, there are recurrent musical references throughout the story; these include a mention of Covent Garden in chapter 4, one of choral music in chapter 5, a suggestion of music that comes from inside Ransom's own body in chapter 8, and a description of a beautiful song that he hears in chapter 15: "Now high in air above him, now welling up as if from glens and valleys far below, it floated through his sleep and was the first sound at every waking. It was formless as the song of a bird, yet it was not a bird's voice. As a bird's voice is to a flute, so this was to a cello: low and ripe and tender, full-bellied, rich and golden-brown: passionate too; but not with the passions of men." The final climactic scene of *Perelandra* was, Lewis said, deliberately "operatic" in its manner of presentation, and so it is highly appropriate that he should have welcomed Donald Swann's idea to compose an opera based on the novel.

The other two references connected with Venus in Lewis's index to volume 5 of his copy of *The Canterbury Tales* are to "Friday," Venus's day (which prompts Lewis to note "From Paxford, a Cotswold man, I have heard 'Friday has a trick above all days'"),[14] and to Venus as ranked among the seven planets of medieval cosmology. I say "medieval cosmology," but, of course, the seven heavens of pre-Copernican astronomy were not a medieval invention; they go back to time immemorial, and Lewis's scholarly interest in Venus finds play in the deepest roots of European mythology as well as in Middle English poetry. However, we cannot here examine his knowledge of Venus's and Aphrodite's many appearances in Roman and Greek mythology, let alone those of Freya or Frigg in Norse mythology. His knowledge of the subject was so extensive and detailed[15] that we must confine our examination to medieval and Renaissance times only.

Venus was prominent in the planetary pantheon partly because she was so bright and beautiful and partly because she could be seen at both dawn and dusk: she was the Morning Star and the Evening Star, both Lucifer and Hesperus. Lewis gives the following brief summary of her qualities in his chapter on the heavens in *The Discarded Image*, his introduction to medieval and Renaissance literature:

> In beneficence Venus stands second only to Jupiter; she is *Fortuna Minor*. Her metal is copper. The connection is not clear till we observe that Cyprus was once famed for its copper mines; that copper is *cyprium*, the Cyprian metal; and that Venus, or Aphrodite, especially worshipped in that island, was κύπρις, the Lady of Cyprus. In mortals she produces beauty and amorousness; in history, fortunate events. Dante makes her sphere the Heaven not, as we might expect from a more obvious poet, of the charitable, but of those, now penitent, who in this life loved greatly and lawlessly.

This summary merely scratches the surface of the topic, however; the Venereal character is, in fact, very considerably more complex, as Lewis well knew. There are various "metaphysical" Venuses distinguishable—but not fully divisible—from the strictly astrological one. To gain a full understanding of how Lewis construed Venereal influence, we need to understand these satellite variants as they supplement and react upon the mother planet.

At the highest level, according to Nicolaus Cusanus, Venus is also a name for God, and Thomas Usk can equate her with "Divine Love."[16] At a slightly lower level, Marsilio Ficino distinguishes two kinds of *Veneres:* the first is the Angelic Mind (*Venus coelistis*), considered in its contemplation of Divine Beauty; the second is the generative power in the *Anima Mundi*—a being inferior to the angels—known as *Venus vulgaris* or *Venus naturalis.*[17] (This second power, the "generative force in nature,"[18] is the same as that which Lewis finds in the *Romance of the Rose,* and also in Lucretius.[19]) In his completion of Christopher Marlowe's "Hero and Leander," George Chapman has a form-giving "archetypal Uranian Venus" that shows him, in Lewis's view, to be "taking his Venus more seriously than Marlowe would have done," despite the fact that "Venus dominates Marlowe's narrative and Saturn that of Chapman."[20] But even Marlowe's Venus is better than Shakespeare's. Lewis considered the Venus of "Venus and Adonis" to be very ill conceived. "This flushed, panting, perspiring, suffocating, loquacious creature," he protested, "is supposed to be the goddess of love herself, the golden Aphrodite. It will not do."[21]

This didactic observation—"It will not do"—indicates that Lewis was beginning to develop an almost proprietorial attitude to Venus and how poets treated her—and, indeed, if we digress from his scholarship for a moment, we can see that Lewis was very keen to show that it was not only Chaucer who could describe himself as Venus's "disciple";[22] Lewis himself was just as devoted to her service.

In his essay "We Have No Right to Happiness," for instance, Lewis argues that unchastity is an evil, not because coitus is an evil, but, on the contrary, because it is good and must be honored: "Foam-born Venus . . . golden Aphrodite . . . Our Lady of Cyprus . . . I never breathed a word against you."[23] He uses *Venus* as a term for the act of sexual intercourse in both *The Pilgrim's Regress* and *The Four Loves,*[24] and in his address "The Inner Ring" he states that virginity ought to be lost "in obedience to Venus" rather than "in obedience to the lure of the caucus."[25] "Aphrodite the laughing" is Homer's formula epithet for the goddess in the *Iliad* and the *Odyssey,* and in Lewis's view, modern discussions of "the act of Venus" "sandpapered most of the Homeric laughter off her face,"[26] turning the most natural and beautiful thing in the world into a terrible pseudoscience that he terms "aphroditology,"[27] an ugly word for an ugly thing, "the one thing venerated in a world without veneration."[28] Lewis was evidently determined to preserve Venus's reputation as the symbolic sponsor of healthy, happy, fertile, and clear-eyed sexuality.

We see how important Venus was to Lewis as an emblem of love in the way that he used her symbolically when writing and speaking about his wife, Joy Davidman. After Joy's death, Lewis published *A Grief Observed*, deriving its title from Christopher Fry's play, *Venus Observed.*[29] And in private conversation, Lewis explicitly likened his wife to Venus, applying to her Percy Shelley's translation of a Platonic epigraph:

> Thou wert my morning star among the living,
> Ere thy fair light had fled;
> Now, having died, thou art as Hesperus giving
> New splendour to the dead.[30]

But we are digressing from his scholarship, and in Lewis's scholarship it is Edmund Spenser who, by quite a large margin, provides him with the richest source of Venereal imagery. Lewis distinguishes the following kinds of Spenserian Venuses: a "Venus-on-earth" (who resembles the second of Ficino's types);[31] a "Venus-as-Paradigma" (who comes from Plato's *Timaeus*);[32] a "Venus-as-planetary-deity" (who is the astrological Intelligence pure and simple);[33] a "bad Venus" (who is Spenser's own picture of diseased sexuality);[34] and a "veiled Venus" (who is to be regarded as one of Spenser's "symbols of God"). This last and divine Venus is "constructed of elements drawn both from Christian revelation and from the intimations of poetic theology." It would give Lewis a good precedent for his own Christian use of Venereal imagery in his poetry and apologetic works.

In Lewis's poetry, Venereal qualities are used only once for obviously Christian purposes. We will examine that occurrence in just a moment, but first we must look at the earliest appearances of Venus in Lewis's published verse, where her qualities serve predominantly as symbols of God's dwelling place in paradise, rather than of God (or Christ) Himself.

When *Spirits in Bondage* was published in 1919, Lewis was not quite sure whether he believed in God or not, but he did believe in (or at any rate longed for) a state that, theologically speaking, he would have been hard-pressed to differentiate from the Heaven of theistic traditions. The volume contains several poems in which Venereal imagery is used to depict an ideal world beyond fear and beyond death. In "The Philosopher," for instance, the poet enquires:

"Who shall cross over for us the bridge of fears / And pass in to the country where the ancient Mothers dwell?" And the answer is not the old man, watery-eyed and full of leaden years, but the young man, "fresh and beautiful of show." It is he who shall "cross at last the shadowy bar / To where the ever-living are." Moreover, it would appear to be this same young man who finally makes that crossing in "Death in Battle":

Open the gates for me,
Open the gates of the peaceful castle, rosy in the West,
In the sweet dim Isle of Apples over the wide sea's breast,
Open the gates for me!

Since elsewhere in *Spirits in Bondage* stars are "isles" (see, for example, the poem "Song"), this "Isle of Apples" is presumably the same Hesperus that has already appeared in the poem of that name. There Lewis presents the same set of images: a western garden beyond the ocean and beyond fear, containing a sacred tree. The poem "Hesperus" does not actually mention that this is an apple tree, but undoubtedly it is so, for this is an early manifestation of Lewis's "Avalon-Hesperides-Western business."[35] Nearly thirty years later, it was still featuring in his poetry. "The Landing" tells of the poet's arrival at the garden of the Hesperides—with its "green hill," its "apple-gold" headlands, its "gum-sweet wood"—and of his dismayed discovery that it is only an imitation: the real Hesperides lies even further to the west.

In his poetic search for the country of the ancient Mothers, Lewis was repeatedly misled by a false trail, which was laid by the "bad Venus" whom he had found in Spenser. Lewis calls her "Venus infernal," and she makes three appearances in his poetry, first in "Wormwood" (1933) ("Venus infernal starving in the strength of fire"), second in "Infatuation" ("Venus infernal taught such voice and eyes / To bear themselves abroad for merchandise"), and third in "Lilith" (1933), a poem about Adam's first wife.[36] She also receives a mention in *The Screwtape Letters* (1942).[37] Under her spell Lewis found that "it was quite easy to think that one desired . . . the garden of Hesperus for the sake of his daughters."[38] But eventually he learned, by means of "discreditable" experience, that this was not the case.[39] In other words, he discovered that *Sehnsucht* was not a disguise of sexual desire. And this was true of the proper expressions of sexual desire as much as the improper ones. Nothing on earth—no appetite of flesh and blood, not even the purest and deepest marital expressions of sexual intercourse—could fully satisfy the longing for the beauty that Venus represents.

This unsatisfiable, inexpressible aspect of Venus is communicated in "The Planets," a poem Lewis wrote in 1935. In his introduction to it, Lewis revealed the high value he attached to the seven heavens of the Ptolemaic cosmos, describing them as "spiritual symbols of permanent value" that were "specially worthwhile" in his own generation.[40] This is how he describes Venus in the poem:

In the third region
VENUS voyages . . . but my voice falters;
Rude rime-making wrongs her beauty,
Whose breasts and brow, and her breath's sweetness
Bewitch the worlds. Wide-spread the reign
Of her secret sceptre, in the sea's caverns,
In grass growing, and grain bursting,
Flower unfolding, and flesh longing,
And shower falling sharp in April.
The metal copper in the mine reddens
With muffled brightness, like muted gold,
By her fingers form'd.

The poet's "voice falters," for "rime-making wrongs her beauty." If we leave Lewis's poetry for a moment, we may find a similar expression of Venus's inexpressible beauty in "The Weight of Glory," a sermon in which Lewis discusses scriptural portrayals of Heaven:

[W]e are to be given the Morning Star [Rev. 2:28]. . . . In one way, of course, God has given us the Morning Star already: you can go and enjoy the gift on many fine mornings if you get up early enough. What more, you may ask, do we want? Ah, but we want so much more. . . . We do not want merely to *see* beauty, though, God knows, even that is bounty enough. We want something else which can hardly be put into words—to be united with the beauty we see, to pass into it, to receive it into ourselves, to bathe in it, to become part of it. . . . That is why the poets tell us such lovely falsehoods. They talk as if the west wind could really sweep into a human soul; but it can't. . . . Or not yet. For if we take the imagery of Scripture seriously, if we believe that God will one day *give* us the Morning Star . . . then we may surmise that both the ancient myths and the modern poetry, so false as history, may be very near the truth as prophecy.[41]

It is highly significant that Lewis should symbolize the human longing for Heaven by means of the Morning Star, for the Morning Star is a biblical title for Christ (2 Pet. 1:19; Rev. 22:16). The fact that Lewis does not mention this in "The Weight of Glory" is itself an aspect of the inexpressibility that he is trying to express, part of the "shyness" that is the theme of that sermon. It is a silence that is audible again in "Five Sonnets," where he writes: "Pitch your demands heaven-high and they'll be met. / Ask for the Morning Star and take (thrown in) / Your earthly love."

"Five Sonnets" makes no attempt to flesh out what it means Christologically to "ask for the Morning Star," and that is to be expected, for if "rime-making" wrongs Venus, it certainly will be insufficient to speak adequately of Christ. Prose, too, is barely sufficient, for this is a subject that "can hardly be put into words." However, Lewis's imagination tended to find prose a more effective vehicle than poetry, and that is certainly the case with his understanding of Venus. And here at last we arrive at *Perelandra,* having almost completed our imaginative voyage to Venus. All that remains is to sketch some of the ways in which Lewis deployed his profound knowledge of and love for Venereal imagery in this beautiful novel of plenitude.

Imaginative Performance in *Perelandra*

In the second volume of the trilogy, Ransom, like St. Paul (in 2 Cor. 12:2), is "taken up to the third heaven."[42] There Ransom "lived and walked on the oceans of the Morning Star," bathing in it, receiving it into himself, becoming part of it. Indeed, he does more than unite himself with Venus; he saves the whole planet from a fall and is given a final resting place there. Perelandra becomes, for Ransom (as we are told in the final chapter), "the Morning Star which He promised to those who conquer."

As well as being a Christological image, *Morning Star* is a biblical term for Babylon and, by traditional extension, for Satan: "How you have fallen from heaven, O morning star, son of the dawn!" (Isa. 14:12a). Lewis taps into this tradition in the portrayal of his own Lucifer, Weston, the great physicist who, after inviting demonic power into himself, becomes "the Un-man." This Un-man has "been with Maleldil in Deep Heaven" and "heard eternal councils." His advent into Perelandra in his spaceship suggests an ejection from the angelic ranks: "like a shooting star something seemed to have streaked across the sky."

The Un-man's temptation of the Green Lady is an outing for the "Venus Infernal" theme, a connection made fairly explicit in chapter 14 where, just before Weston is finally dispatched, he climbs out of the realm of "infernal fire." Well before that point, though, Weston has shown himself to belong to the dark side of Venus: whereas the celestial Venus is the source of all life, of which human life is the created crown, Weston is host to the Un-man. Venus has a word of blessing for everything that is good; Weston has one word that he prizes above all others: *nothing*. He has come, he says, to bring Perelandra "death in abundance," a blasphemous parody of John 10:10: "I have come that you might have life; life in abundance." Weston would bring the Green Lady's world to nothing, and in the attempt he keeps trying to poison Tinidril's imagination (the first step in undermining her will) by telling her tales of tragic heroines who had been "oppressed by fathers, cast off by husbands, deserted by lovers"—female martyrs who, if men had had their way, would have been kept down "to mere child-bearing." The picture he paints is "always very nearly true." But not quite. In fact, in ordinary terrestrial speech, these heroines were "witches or perverts," more reminiscent of "Agrippina and of Lady Macbeth" than of noble pioneers.

Having failed to corrupt Tinidril's imagination through words, the Unman attempts the same thing by means of visual images. In parody of the ancient mythological image of Aphrodite's looking glass, he produces a small "English pocket mirror that might have cost three-and-six." This, he promises, enables one "to walk alongside oneself as if one were a second person and to delight in one's own beauty. Mirrors were made to teach this art." As it turns out, Tinidril is only frightened, not corrupted, by the sight of her own face, and Ransom eventually perceives that the Un-man's strategy is to awaken in her mind not vanity concerning her physical beauty but egoism concerning her beautiful soul. Not that consciousness of one's own beauty is portrayed by Lewis as an evil. On the contrary, Maleldil has already provided for Tinidril a way of seeing herself in the reflection from the sky, a phenomenon observable "three days out of five in the planet of love. The queen of those seas views herself continually in a celestial mirror."

In any event, Weston's strategy does not work; the Un-man fails to infect Perelandra with the spirit of Venus Infernal, and the abiding impression left by the book is not these temptations but the almost overwhelming sensuous richness of the planet itself. As mentioned earlier, the plenitude at the heart of this book is different from an undifferentiated "everything-ism'"; the fullness of life that Venus inspires is not blandly monistic but instead has a positive and distinct quality. In part, this distinct quality is conveyed by certain recurrent images: sweetness, laughter, copper, apples, and warm wetness, to name but a few of them.[43] In part also, it is conveyed by showing us that bad thing (Venus Infernal), which can be parasitic on the true Venus and which has to be destroyed for Venus to be truly herself. One particular aspect of the anti-Venus impulse is fear. The conquering of fear is especially Venereal for "perfect love casts out fear" (1 John 4:18). When Tinidril for the first time sees her face in Weston's mirror, a new expression comes over her face:

> It was as easy to read as that of a man in a shelter when a bomb is coming.
> "What is it?" she repeated.
> "It is called Fear," said Weston's mouth. Then the creature turned its face full on Ransom and grinned.
> "Fear," she said. "This is Fear," pondering the discovery; then, with abrupt finality, "I do not like it."
> "It will go away," said the Un-man, when Ransom interrupted.
> "It will never go away if you do what he wishes. It is into more and more fear that he is leading you."

It is this conquering of fear that we see also in the first chapter, as the narrator makes his way to Ransom's cottage, a powerful and memorable opening episode that strikes the chord for this leitmotif; there is to be no fear on the planet of love, because fear has to do with punishment—that is to say, with privation. But there are to be no privations in this land of profusion: that would be a contradiction in terms. The love of money, we are reminded, is the root of all evil, and money is valued as a means of ar-resting the unrolling of the film, of controlling one's life, in a way that runs counter to the planet's spirit of superfluity and supererogation. Gratuity, by definition, is something that money cannot buy; and the plenteousness of Venus is, Ransom finds, not only unbought but even unsought: it is all gift.

Another particularly notable way in which Lewis conveys the idea of gift is through the imagery of apples. The paradise that is Perelandra is different from the paradise that is the Garden of Eden. Ransom recognizes that he has arrived at the real "Garden of the Hesperides," and although Eve and her apple are several times mentioned or alluded to, this story is the reverse of the Genesis myth: it is Eden without the Fall. Perelandra is the "apple-laden land" of Euripides[44] in which a "Fixed Land," rather than a forbidden fruit, represents the divine command, and apples have no prohibitory significance. They feature most obviously under the guise of the "gourds" and the "bubble trees" that Ransom both freely enjoys and freely abstains from; also, at one remove, as breasts. Apples, as Lewis wrote elsewhere, "often symbolize the female breasts":[45] here, in a profound remythologizing of the Eden apple, Ransom is "breast-fed by the planet Venus herself."

Freudian interpretations of literature have been so abused by lazy critics that one hesitates to comment further on the sexual symbolism inherent in the novel. However, in a work so avowedly Venereal, we should, of course, expect the presence of sexual elements, for this is part and parcel of Lewis's total purpose in *Perelandra*: not just setting his plot on the planet of love, but infusing its quality into the narrative itself. Ransom's overcoming of the Un-man in the caves of Perelandra, after which he is "almost too weak to move," but not too weak to enjoy "rich clusters of grape-like fruit," when "eating passed into sleeping by a transition he could never remember," is one noteworthy instantiation of this idea.[46] Another is to be found in the following two paragraphs, reflecting something of the peculiar qualities of Mars and Venus respectively:

> He has immeasurable use for each thing that is made, that His love and splendour may flow forth like a strong river which has need of a great watercourse and fills alike the deep pools and the little crannies, that are filled equally and remain unequal; and when it has filled them brimful it flows over and makes new channels. We also have need beyond measure of all that He has made. Love me, my brothers, for I am infinitely necessary to you and for your delight I was made. Blessed be He!

> He has no need at all of anything that is made. An eldil is not more needful to Him than a grain of the Dust: a peopled world no more needful than a world that is empty: but all needless alike, and what all add to Him is nothing. We also have no need of anything that is made. Love me, my brothers, for I am infinitely superfluous, and your love shall be like His, born neither of your need nor of my deserving, but a plain bounty. Blessed be He!

We have here an antithesis: the necessary and the superfluous. And we may rightly see in this antithesis a reflection of the antithesis that has been established over the entire course of the first two books in the Ransom Trilogy, the antithesis between masculine and feminine that will be resolved in the third book, *That Hideous Strength,* whose very first word, *matrimony,*[47] indicates what its main theme is to be. Malacandra, the masculine planet, is Mars, and Mars, as Lewis wrote in his poem "The Planets," is "necessity's son": "Love me, my brothers, for I am infinitely necessary." But Perelandra, the feminine planet, has a quality that is different from necessity and which is all the more beautiful for that: "Love me, my brothers, for I am infinitely superfluous, and your love shall be like His, born neither of your need nor of my deserving, but a plain bounty." Just as that which balances, faces, and completes masculinity is femininity, so that which balances, faces, and completes necessity is superfluity, abundance, plenitude, or, as Lewis puts it, "a plain bounty."

It should not surprise us, therefore, that the final chapter of the third volume in the trilogy is entitled "Venus at St Anne's."[48] Perelandra, the planet of love, lingers on Earth and inspires all the virtuous couples to imitate her ways by making love—not just the human couples (the Dimbles, Dennistons, Maggses, and Studdocks), but also the animals, two by two (the bats, bears, elephants, hedgehogs, horses, jackdaws, mice).[49] One of Lewis's favorite medieval paintings was, as noted above, Botticelli's "Mars and Venus." It depicts the typical medieval literary theme of the proud young man (Bayard, Troilus) tamed by Venus,[50] and to just such a scene the whole trilogy has been leading, the connubial reunion of Mars and Venus as reflected in the mundane marriage of Mark and Jane Studdock. And, in a brilliant twist, it is Jane whose love is shown to be most god-like—that is to say, most masculine—at the very end.

In the final scene of *That Hideous Strength,* it is Mark who adopts the traditional feminine role of passivity. He has taken off his clothes and is waiting in the bedroom of the lodge for his wife to arrive. When Jane turns up, she stands "with one hand on the latch" (like the bridegroom in the *Song of Solomon*) and hesitates, thinking about what she should do: "Still she did not move the latch. Then she noticed that the window, the bedroom window, was open. Clothes were piled on the chair inside the room so carelessly that they lay over the sill: the sleeve of a shirt—Mark's shirt—even hung over down the outside wall. And in all this damp too. How exactly like Mark! Obviously it was high time she went in."

It is Jane who "goes in" to her husband, not the other way round. She adopts the traditional masculine role of entering because she has become more truly a disciple of divine love (as symbolized by Venus) than Mark has. Mark is a child of Mars (his very name indicates that), "necessity's son." Necessity and bounty meet in this closing scene, and bounty (so we are given to understand) will gently, irresistibly overcome necessity. Botticelli's picture, which Lewis so liked to meditate upon, shows Mars embracing his blessed defeat, enjoying the sweet sleep that comes after love, while Venus, awake, yet restful and serene, looks calmly and steadily upon him.

And it is this kind of postcoital repletion, as signified both by the needful sleep of Mars and by the wakeful bounty of Venus, that I think Lewis is symbolizing in the operatic finale at the climax of *Perelandra*, during which Ransom has a vision of a great cosmic dance, a vision which culminates as follows:

> And by now the thing must have passed altogether out of the region of sight as we understand it. For [Ransom] says that the whole solid figure of these enamoured and inter-inanimated circlings was suddenly revealed as the mere superficies of a far vaster pattern in four dimensions, and that figure as the boundary of yet others in other worlds: till suddenly as the movement grew yet swifter, the interweaving yet more ecstatic, the relevance of all to all yet more intense, as dimension was added to dimension and that part of him which could reason and remember was dropped farther and farther behind that part of him which saw, even then, at the very zenith of complexity, complexity was eaten up and faded, as a thin white cloud fades into the hard blue burning of the sky, and a simplicity beyond all comprehension, ancient and young as spring, illimitable, pellucid, drew him with cords of infinite desire into its own stillness. He went up into such a quietness, a privacy, and a freshness that at the very moment when he stood farthest from our ordinary mode of being he had the sense of stripping off encumbrances and awaking from trance, and coming to himself.

Too many studies of *Perelandra* have focused on the superficially biblical properties of the novel (the naked lady, the apples, the state of innocence, the temptations), without showing an awareness of the Venereal imagery that underlies the whole subcreated world. The fundamental message of *Perelandra* and, indeed, of the entire trilogy, is not, I believe, located in specific parallels to certain scriptural passages: it is to be read off the entire form and content of the story. Love never sleeps—that is the theological truth to which Lewis's imaginative involvement with Venus drives him. Human beings, in his view, exist not primarily to love God but to be loved by God, to be adored by the One who neither slumbers nor sleeps.[51] The mortal necessity in man needs to be "brought to bed of Love,"[52] and "when I wake up after Thy image, I shall be satisfied," as Ransom says to himself at the start of chapter 12, quoting Psalm 17:15. That psalm and certain other biblical sources—"I sleep, but my heart waketh" (Song of Sol. 5:2), "We love Him because He first loved us" (1 John 4:19), "Plenteousness within Thy palaces" (Ps. 122:7), "Come unto me . . . and I will give you rest" (Matt. 11:28),—are much more pertinent scriptural bases for Lewis's meaning in *Perelandra*, I submit, than the ostensibly relevant Genesis connotations.

The bridegroom's embraces do not tire. The wheat is pressed down and running over. The cornucopia can never be exhausted.

Notes

This essay is derived in part from my *Planet Narnia: The Seven Heavens in the Imagination of C. S. Lewis* (New York: Oxford Univ. Press, 2008).

1. In my view, the trilogy should be called the Cosmic Trilogy or the Ransom Trilogy, not the Space Trilogy. In *Out of the Silent Planet,* Lewis writes, "'Space' seemed a blasphemous libel . . . Space was the wrong word . . . If we could even effect in one per cent of our readers a change-over from the conception of Space to the conception of Heaven, we should have made a beginning." C. S. Lewis, *OSP* (London: Pan, 1983), 35, 180.

2. Ransom's experiences of prodigal generosity on Perelandra are anticipated in his reception, like "a second Danae," of sidereal influences at the start of the first novel: see Lewis, *OSP,* 34.

3. Per Lewis, *OSP,* 201.

4. C. S. Lewis to Arthur Greeves, Feb. 20, 1917, in Lewis, *CL* I (London: HarperCollins, 2000), 282.

5. C. S. Lewis to Arthur Greeves, Feb. 12, 1918, in Lewis, *CL* I, 355.

6. See Lewis's letter to W. H. Lewis, his brother, Dec. 22, 1914; and his letters to Arthur Greeves, May 4 and 11, 1915, in Lewis, *CL* I, 96, 115, 118; W. H. Lewis, *Brothers and Friends: The Diaries of Major Warren Hamilton Lewis,* ed. Clyde S. Kilby and Marjorie Lamp Mead (San Francisco, Calif: Harper & Row, 1982), 169.

7. See C. S. Lewis to Arthur Greeves, May 5, 1919, in Lewis, *CL* I, 446. Com-

pare with the entry of May 26, 1923, in the unpublished work "The Lewis Papers: Memoirs of the Lewis Family, 1850–1930," ed. W. H. Lewis, held in the Wade Collection, Wheaton College, Wheaton, Ill.

8. Derek Brewer, "The Tutor: A Portrait," in *C. S. Lewis at the Breakfast Table and Other Reminiscences*, ed. James T. Como (London: Collins, 1980), 56. There he also had Tintoretto's "The Origin of the Milky Way"; see Peter Bayley, "From Master to Colleague," in Como, *Breakfast Table*, 77.

9. "One of the pictures Lewis most cared for when he first visited the National Gallery in 1922," Alastair Fowler, "C. S. Lewis: Supervisor," *Yale Review* 91, no. 4 (Oct. 2003): 64–80.

10. George Watson, "The Art of Disagreement: C. S. Lewis (1898–1963)," *The Hudson Review* (1995): 229–39, 233. Lewis is referring to the Warburg Institute in London, the incomparable archive of iconography.

11. C. S. Lewis to Arthur Greeves, May 5, 1919, and to Leo Baker, Feb. 25, 1921, in Lewis, *CL* I, 447 and 521 respectively.

12. C. S. Lewis to W. H. Lewis, Apr. 21, 1940, in Lewis, *CL* II (London: Harper-Collins, 2004), 397.

13. The author thanks Bernard O'Donoghue, Fellow in English at Wadham College, Oxford, the owner of the volumes, for kindly loaning them for inspection.

14. Lewis's copy of *The Complete Works of Geoffrey Chaucer*, ed. W. W. Skeat (Oxford: Clarendon, 1899) 4: 45. Fred Paxford was Lewis's gardener at the Kilns.

15. See, for example, within his published diaries alone, C. S. Lewis, *AMR* (London: HarperCollins, 1991), 297, 346, 395.

16. C. S. Lewis, *SIL* (Cambridge, UK: Cambridge Univ. Press, 1967), 16; C. S. Lewis, *AOL* (Oxford: Oxford Univ. Press, 1958), 225.

17. Lewis, *SIL*, 50–51; cf. C. S. Lewis, *EL* (Oxford: Clarendon Press, 1954), 374–75.

18. Lewis, *AOL*, 121.

19. C. S. Lewis, *SIW* (Cambridge, UK: Cambridge Univ. Press, 1990), 225.

20. C. S. Lewis, "Hero and Leander," in his *SLE* (Cambridge, UK: Cambridge Univ. Press, 1980), 70.

21. Lewis, *EL*, 498–99. Cf. Lewis, "Hero and Leander," 59.

22. See C. S. Lewis, "What Chaucer really did to *Il Filostrato*," in his *SLE*, 28.

23. C. S. Lewis, "We Have No Right to Happiness," in his *Essay Collection and Other Short Pieces*, ed. Lesley Walmsley (London: HarperCollins, 2000), 390; ellipses in original.

24. C. S. Lewis, *PR* (Glasgow: Fount, 1980), 110; C. S. Lewis, *FL* (Glasgow: Collins, 1991), 85.

25. C. S. Lewis, "The Inner Ring," in his *Essay Collection and Other Short Pieces*, ed. Lesley Walmsley (London: HarperCollins, 2000), 724.

26. C. S. Lewis, *LTM* (London: Collins, 1983), 16.

27. "C. S. Lewis, interviewed by Wayland Young," *Journal of Inklings Studies*, vol. 1, no. 1, 23. Cf. "horrid Aphrodite mysticism," C. S. Lewis to Ruth Pitter, Aug. 31, 1948, in Lewis, *CL* II, 875.

28. C. S. Lewis, "Miracles," in his *Essay Collection and Other Short Pieces*, ed. Lesley Walmsley (London: HarperCollins, 2000), 112. *Veneration* is, of course, etymologically related to *Venus*. Let the reader understand.

29. This, at any rate, is the view of his Oxford contemporary, A. L. Rowse; see *The Diaries of A. L. Rowse*, ed. Richard Ollard (London: Penguin, 2003), 365.

30. See George Sayer, *Jack: C. S. Lewis and His Times* (San Francisco, Calif.: Harper & Row, 1988), 251.

31. Lewis, *SIL*, 51.

32. Lewis, *SIL*, 49; cf. Lewis, *EL*, 375.

33. Lewis, *SIL*, 49.

34. Lewis, *AOL*, 332.

35. Lewis, *AMR*, 314. Cf. C. S. Lewis, *SBJ* (Glasgow: Collins, 1982), 140, 165; also C. S. Lewis, *NP* (London: HarperCollins, 1994), 4, where Lewis mentions the "Hesperian or Western Garden" system of imagery that he "mainly derived from Euripedes, Milton, Morris, and the early Yeats." The Hesperides were the daughters of Hesperus, god of the evening star, who guarded the grove of immortality-giving apple trees in Hera's western orchard and who occasionally plucked fruit for themselves. Not trusting them, Hera placed in the garden an unsleeping, hundred-headed dragon named Ladon.

36. Cf. C. S. Lewis to Barfield, June 19, 1930, in Lewis, *CL* I, 904; C. S. Lewis to Greeves, Sept. 1, 1933, in Lewis, *CL* II, 119–20; C. S Lewis, *THS* (London: Pan, 1983), 62–63.

37. Screwtape tells Wormwood: "You will find, if you look carefully into any human's heart, that he is haunted by at least two imaginary women—a terrestrial and an infernal Venus." C. S. Lewis, *SL* (Glasgow: Collins, 1982), 104.

38. Lewis, *SBJ*, 137.

39. Lewis would have acknowledged that "discreditable" expressions of Venus (in his case, he means masturbation and his early affair with Mrs. Moore) were not full tests of *sehnsucht*. Marriage, on the other hand, was. However, this, too, could not test it to destruction. See C. S. Lewis, *AGO* (London: Faber & Faber, 1966), 9: "We both knew we wanted something besides one another."

40. C. S. Lewis, "The Alliterative Metre," in Lewis, *SLE*, 24.

41. C. S. Lewis, "The Weight of Glory," in Lewis, *Essay Collection and Other Short Pieces*, ed. Lesley Walmsley (London: HarperCollins, 2000), 104.

42. In Jewish thought, the heavens were sometimes divided into three and sometimes seven. See *The Testament of Levi*, 2:7; *Assumption of Isaiah*, 6:13; Babylonian Talmud, *Hagigah* 12b. Cf. 1 Kgs 8:27; Eph. 4:10.

43. As regards sweetness, Lewis gives us "a light wind, full of sweetness," "sweet heather," "sweet new scents," "sweet night breezes." As regards laughter, he tells us that Perelandran thunder is "the laugh, rather than the roar, of heaven"; Ransom suffers "a real schoolboy fit of the giggles"; the Green Lady bursts "into laughter—peal upon peal of laughter till her whole body shook with it"; "her sudden laughter"; she "laughed for a whole minute on end"; "the King laughed . . . Ransom laughed . . . the

Queen laughed as well. And the birds began clapping their wings and the beasts wagging their tails." As regards Venus's metal, he mentions a "copper-coloured floor," a "copper-coloured ridge," "copper-coloured heather," the "coppery-green of the water," the "coppery sea." And as regards warmth and wetness, Ransom's first experience of the planet is of "unconsciously" swimming in an ocean which is "as warm as a shallow bay with sandy bottom in a sub-tropical climate"; he is "naked yet warm"; "the darkness was warm"; there is "warm splendour" all over Perelandra, the planet on which "the lands swim"; the Green Lady, Ransom speculates, has "a marine ancestry"—naturally, because she is the foam-born goddess. C. S. Lewis, *Perelandra* (London: Pan, 1983), passim.

44. Euripides: *Hippolytus*, 1:742; cf. C. S. Lewis, *TWHF* (Glasgow: Collins, 1985), 17. In *THS*, Perelandra becomes Avalon (*Abhal* means "apple" in Gaelic), though Lewis spells it variously as *Abhalljin* and *Aphallin* in that novel. Ransom returns permanently to Perelandra at the end of *THS*, joining Arthur, the Pendragon, who "sleeps far hence in Avalon." C. S. Lewis, "Victory" in *CP* (London: Fount HarperCollins, 1994), 170.

45. C. S. Lewis, "Spenser's Cruel Cupid," in his *SMRL* (Cambridge, UK: Cambridge Univ. Press, 1966), 166. For more on Hesperian apples, see C. S. Lewis to Ruth Pitter, Mar. 5, 1955, in Lewis, *CL* III (London: HarperCollins, 2006).

46. Ransom learns war fully in the sphere of Venus (*THS*, 274) and it is his "long struggle in the caves of Perelandra" that comes back to him when Mars descends in *THS*. We might have expected this struggle to have happened on Malacandra, and to explain this apparent inconsistency we must recall that "in a certain juncture of the planets each may play the other's part." C. S. Lewis to A. K. Hamilton Jenkin, Nov. 4, 1925, in Lewis, *CL* I, 653. We also must recall that the trilogy is largely concerned with the acquisition of true masculinity and true femininity. Mythologically, Lewis seems to be suggesting that masculinity is only fully learned in relation to femininity. Deep in the "caves" of Venus, stricken with pain, as the Malacandrian Oyarsa had foretold (Lewis, *OSP*, 166), Ransom overcomes the Un-man, giving of himself for the life of the planet, and so realizes what it is to be a man.

47. Literally, "mother-making." Jane Studdock is to become a mother and bear the new Pendragon who will save Logres from disaster. Motherhood and motherliness are key aspects of Venus's nature, as Lewis understands it. In *Perelandra* we are told that the Un-man existed "before the mothers of the mothers of [Ransom's] mother were conceived." Ransom's own name was planned to yield a new meaning "before his Mother had borne him, before his ancestors had been called Ransoms." He warns the Green Lady about "mothers wearing themselves to a ravelling." She, he learns, has no human mother because, as she says, "I *am* the Mother" (Lewis, *Perelandra*, passim).

48. St. Anne is traditionally thought to have been the mother of the Lord's mother, the Blessed Virgin Mary. However, Lewis claimed to have selected St. Anne's "merely as a plausible and euphonious name," not for any deeper reason. C. S. Lewis to William Kinter, July 30, 1954, in Lewis, *CL* III, 497. If this is an accurate recollection on

Lewis's part, the choice was a happy one. As Sanford Schwartz points out, "Marina Warner's intriguing account of the cult of St. Anne in seventeenth-century France (the specialty of Lewis's older brother) suggests some of the reasons that Lewis may have chosen the name: 'Anne's story echoes biblical tales of barrenness reversed by God as a special sign of his favour to the parents and a singular benediction on their late, longed-for offspring . . . Anne was seen above all as a patroness of childless women and grandmothers.'" Warner, quoted in Sanford Schwartz, *C. S. Lewis on the Final Frontier: Science and the Supernatural in the Space Trilogy* (New York: Oxford Univ. Press, 2009), 187.

49. "Venus causes all animals to procreate their *saecula*" (Lewis, *SIW*, 225).

50. Lewis, *AOL*, 76.

51. "To please God . . . to be a real ingredient in the divine happiness . . . to be loved by God, not merely pitied, but delighted in as an artist delights in his work or a father in a son—it seems impossible, a weight or burden of glory which our thoughts can hardly sustain. But so it is." C. S. Lewis, "The Weight of Glory," in Lewis, *EC* II, 102.

52. Lewis, *PR*, 233.

"For the Dance All Things Were Made"

The Great Dance in C. S. Lewis's Perelandra

PAUL S. FIDDES

At the end of C. S. Lewis's novel *Perelandra*, his hero Ransom has a whole year to gaze at a vision of the Great Dance. In the briefer time it will take to read this essay, I hope to open up some of the wonders of this cosmic dance. For it *is* extraordinary. In its context it sums up the themes of the novel, but it also uncovers the depths of Lewis's religious vision of the universe. Beginning with a hymn of praise and culminating in the vision itself, this portrayal of the Great Dance is not the medieval commonplace so often suggested—that is, just a picture of the universe as sharing in a dance around its center, God. Something more startling is happening in Lewis's version of the Great Dance, something that shows the creativity of Lewis's thought and that might prompt us to creative thinking in our turn.

THE CENTER THAT MOVES

The first, and perhaps the most important, aspect of the Great Dance to which I want to draw attention is this: it has a center that moves.

To understand the significance of this, we need to start where Ransom starts, with a question: who and what is at the center of the presence and attention of Maleldil? (Maleldil is, of course, a name for God in Lewis's mythology.) Who is in the inner circle, the "inner ring"?[1] The hymn and the vision are prompted by the disclosure to Ransom that his planet, Earth, will be delivered from its bondage to dark powers as a preparation for a new beginning of creation. Far from being the "last things," as Earthly theologians name the event, this redemption of the Earth from its Dark Lord will not even be the *beginning* of all things, but only the wiping out of a false start, mere prologue to the beginning.[2] Ransom is deeply troubled, because this perspective on time and space seems to him to thrust his world into a remote corner of the universe, where he was used to thinking that the coming down of Maleldil to Earth as a man "is the central happening of all that happens" (*P*, 245). This disclosure seems to Ransom not only to displace the Earth from the center but to open up a meaningless universe with no center at all, only millions of worlds that lead nowhere. Any hope of a plan or pattern seems to be an optical illusion, a trick of the eyes.

The picture of the Great Dance counters this nihilism. In the dance, declare mysterious voices, *every* participant is at the center (*P*, 249), and the pattern of the dance can be seen as the movement of each entity becomes in turn "the breaking into flower of the whole design" (*P*, 250). This is because God is the center and God is everywhere: "Each grain is at the centre. The Dust is at the centre. The Worlds are at the centre. The beasts are at the centre. The ancient peoples are there. The race that sinned is there . . . the gods are there also. Blessed be He! Where Maleldil is, there is the centre. He is in every place. . . . Because we are with him, each of us is at the centre . . . there seems no centre because it is all centre . . ." (*P*, 249, 251). We cannot miss the echo of the medieval saying that "God is an intelligible sphere whose centre is everywhere and circumference nowhere." We find this sentence in Bonaventure, who is quoting from Alan of Lille.[3] Lewis backs up this omnipresence of the center by affirming that God is *in* all things, and all things are in God: "He dwells (all of Him dwells) within the seed of the smallest flower and is not cramped: Deep Heaven is inside Him who is inside the seed and does not distend Him. Blessed be He!" (*P*, 247).

This view of the relation of God to the world may be called *panentheism*—everything *in* God—which must not be confused with *pantheism*—everything *as* God. Similarly, Bonaventure follows his statement about God as the center by declaring that God as most perfect and immense "is within all things, but not as included in them, and outside of all things, but not as excluded from them."[4]

Certainly then, Lewis's picture of the Great Dance combines transcendence with immanence, eternity with time. But something even more extraordinary is happening here. He is merging two images—the cosmic dance and the universal indwelling of the center. Both images in Christian tradition assume that the center is *unmoving*, in accord with Aristotle's definition of the Unmoved Mover,[5] assumed (though with qualification) by Plotinus.[6] According to the traditional image of the dance, angels, planets, and other created beings circle around the still center of God, moving around a God who is unmoving in a Neoplatonic stasis.[7] God moves all things but remains motionless as God's self. As Lewis summarizes the medieval tradition in his book *The Discarded Image*, "There must in the last resort be something which, *motionless itself*, initiates the motion of all other things."[8] In a Neoplatonist universe, indebted to both Aristotle and Plato, God, or "the One" as pure Being, cannot share in the qualities of a world of becoming and change. Further, according to the image of the center that is everywhere, God can be in all time and space just because God is eternal and unmoving. As Bonaventure puts it, pure and absolute Being "comprises and enters all durations, as if existing at the same time as their centre and circumference, because it is eternal and most present"; quoting Boethius, he goes on to say "Because it is . . . most immutable, for that reason 'remaining at rest [*stabilis manens*] it grants motion to everything else.'"[9] The images of both dance and omnipresent center have thus traditionally relied upon the conviction that the center of the dance does not move, but when Lewis brings them *together* here they make a different imaginative impact. The impression made on us is that the center of the dance is itself dancing. We are not just witnessing a dance *around* God, but the dance *of* God. Lewis's version of the Great Dance is not merely an "updated form of Christian Neoplatonism,"[10] or a medieval commonplace. It deconstructs Neoplatonism while using its images.

Admittedly, the hymn and the vision only *imply* that the primal dance is Maleldil *himself*. Lewis writes that his "love and splendour flow forth like a strong river . . . [making] new channels," so that the patterns of the dance are the passionate energies of God. Such are the imaginative effects of bringing together the cosmic dance and a universal mutual inwelling between creation and creator. However, there is much else in Lewis that supports this understanding of the dance, *so* much else in fact that some commentators on Lewis simply assume that the Great Dance of Perelandra is led by Maleldil as master of the revels and the supreme Dancer,[11] and so they miss the extraordinary reversal of thought and imagination that is going on.

Later, Lewis expresses his dissatisfaction with the conventional account of the cosmic dance in *The Discarded Image*. He sets out the medieval world order in which each planetary sphere, or something resident in it, is a conscious intelligence moved by intellectual love of God through the activity of the *Primum Mobile*, the First Moveable.[12] The *Primum Mobile* is moved by its love for God (the Primal Mover) and so communicates motion to the rest of the universe. God, while utterly motionless, initiates the motion of all other things, because they are moved by the object of their love. It is like, we may say, a beautiful girl or man setting a whole room of people in motion around him or her, while remaining stationary in the middle, toying with a glass of wine. Lewis himself opts for the image of a moth fluttering round a candle flame (*DI*, 119). The first to be moved, and then to move others, is the *Primum Mobile*, and Lewis refers to "one old picture" in which the intelligence of the First Moveable is represented as a girl dancing and playing with her sphere as a ball (*DI*, 119);[13] she is the leader of the dance, the swiftest mover and shaker. I want to return to this picture shortly. The key thing is that the dancers are the First Moveable and then the other spheres, but not God, who is the still center of the turning worlds.[14] Elsewhere in *The Discarded Image*, Lewis refers to the dance of the angels in Pseudo-Dionysius's treatise *The Celestial Hierarchy*[15] and notes that Dante has something similar.[16] Dionysius envisages a threefold hierarchy of dancing celestial choirs, moving in distinct patterns around God, providing a spiritual ladder of ascent for the soul to approach God. But Lewis explains the reason why, in his view, the picture of the cosmic dance of the spheres generally failed to grip the imaginations of Christian spiritual writers in the Middle Ages; it is too static, he urges, since God is not just the passive object of love but the active lover, the Good Shepherd who goes out to seek the lost sheep (*DI*, 113–14, 120).

Long before writing *The Discarded Image* (1964), and at about the same time as writing *Perelandra* (1943), Lewis had already articulated a more dynamic understanding of the dance. The dance of heaven in which the creation participates is not merely that of the ranks of angels, but that of the triune God. In *Beyond Personality* (1944), he writes "In Christianity God is not a static thing—not even a person—but a dynamic, pulsating activity, a life, almost a kind of drama. Almost, if you will not think me irreverent, a kind of *dance.* . . . The whole dance, or drama, or pattern of this three-Personal life is to be played out in each one of us: or (putting it the other way round) each one of us has got to enter that pattern, take his place in that dance."[17] Lewis here makes the acute theological point that God is not an object to be observed but a reality to be engaged in. The image of dance is an image of participation, and it is the *experimental* aspect of talking about God that interests Lewis.[18] He admits that language of the Trinity is difficult; indeed a three-personal God cannot be imagined or pictured in the mind even with the help of analogies. This Lewis sees not as a disadvantage but as a positive advantage, writing, "You may ask, 'If we cannot imagine a three-personal Being, what is the good of talking about him?' Well, there isn't any good talking *about* him. The thing that matters is actually being drawn into that three-personal life, and that may begin any time—tonight if you like" (*MC*, 129; emphasis added). By speaking of God as "beyond personality" but not as impersonal, Lewis is recognizing a necessary apophaticism—a negative way—in all theological language. We might say that the very elusiveness of the picture of the divine dance in *Perelandra,* implied through the bringing together of two images, illustrates that the dance cannot be observed or even imagined but only participated in.

Arriving at the Idea of the Dance of God

I have already mentioned that writers on Lewis fail to notice the breach with the medieval world-picture that he makes with his picture of a dancing God, a moving center. Since the early 1980s or so, the image of the divine life as a dance has become increasingly popular. It is common for religious writers of the present day to refer to the ancient notion of *perichoresis*—the interweaving of three persons in God—with the image of the dance.[19] Some notice that there is a play on words taking place here: *perichoresis* derives from *perichoreo,* meaning "to interpenetrate," which sounds similar to another verb, *perichoreuo* meaning "to dance around." The mutual indwelling of the persons and movement in and through each other may thus be pictured as a kind of round-dance. However, there is no evidence that this association was made in theology of the Trinity until the modern period, despite the fact that some writers simply assume that *perichoresis* can be translated as "a dance." In fact, it is difficult to find an unambiguous reference to the Trinity as a dance in Christian thinking earlier than Lewis himself.

Of course, the spheres, angels, and other beings dance around God, as we have seen. As well as envisaging all created intelligences as held together in a dance, Plotinus depicts the soul that has looked on the One as now dancing around Him, the fount of goodness.[20] In the Christian version, there is a "never-ending dance" of the angels around the throne of God, in which Christians may aspire to participate in eternity; according to Basil the Great, Christians at worship here and now may imitate the ring-dance (*choreia*) of heaven in their prayers and hymns to the creator.[21] In addition to the dancing angels of Pseudo-Dionysius, we may mention the dance of the Church Doctors in the sun that Dante sees in the *Paradiso.*[22] The picture persists from the Middle Ages to the Elizabethan era: in Sir John Davies's poem, *Orchestra; or, A Poem on Dancing* (1596), all everyday actions are included in the dance, including the fluttering of Penelope's eyelashes, and the dancing of the point of a needle as she sews. When Antinous, in the poem, asks Penelope to dance, he invites her to participate in the heavenly dance, to "imitate heaven whose beauties excellent / Are in continual motion day and night."[23]

The activity of Christ on Earth is depicted as a dance in several texts, among them the second-century Gnostic *Hymn of Jesus,*[24] when Jesus declares to his disciples at the Last Supper, "I am the Word who did dance all things. . . . 'Twas I who leapt and danced." The medieval English carol "Tomorrow Will Be My Dancing Day" depicts the birth, baptism, temptation, and passion of Christ as a dance, with the aim "to call my true love [i.e., the human soul] to my dance." But this does not exactly express the dance of God: the emphasis is strongly on the humanity of Christ, not on the eternal divine nature. It is Christ as man who dances:

> Then was I born of a virgin pure,
> Of her I took fleshly substance;
> Thus was I knit to man's nature
> To call my true love to my dance.[25]

It seems, then, that Lewis himself has converted the dance of Plotinus and Pseudo-Dionysius into a dance of the Trinity. This may be because—as he himself indicates—he has a strong sense of participation in God, and of the generous actions of God as lover of creation, not just as its beloved. However, other factors may well have influenced him. Among them was, perhaps, his reading of Henri Bergson, for which Sanford Schwartz has made a strong case. According to Schwartz, Bergson promotes an "inversion of Platonism,"[26] in which the world is no longer envisaged as a system of unchanging forms perceived by the intellect but as a process of perpetual becoming, given to us in the stream of experience. Despite Lewis's negative judgments on Bergson and his dismissal of the "life-force philosophy," Schwartz demonstrates that the very landscape of Perelandra is shaped by Bergson's dynamic naturalism. Lewis reverses the traditional concept of paradise as an immutable state that precedes a lapse into time and change, and instead presents it as a perpetual flux.[27] The Green Lady rejoices in the distinctive character of each phase of the creation as it unfolds in time, greeting each wave of time and circumstance as it rolls toward her. The temptation she must resist is to stay on the fixed land, which symbolizes the desire to control experience by fixing it into something she can possess.

Ransom's own experience on Perelandra begins with temptations to immobilize the flux. As he tastes the delicious fruit of Perelandra, or bathes in the bursting fruit of the bubble-tree, he overcomes the impulse to repeat a pleasurable experience, reflecting "the itch to have things over again, as if life were a film that could be unrolled twice, or even made to work backwards. . . . was it possibly the root of all evil"? (*P,* 54).[28] So Edward, in Narnia, finds that he always craves more of the White Witch's Turkish delight.[29] Resisting the temptation to repeat a pleasure is partly a matter of obedience to God, a willingness to receive what God gives in each new moment, but it is also a decision to live in accord with a world that—in a Bergsonian way—is always in the process of development. The hymn that begins the Great Dance celebrates a vision of creative evolution that matches the need to throw oneself into the new wave that Maleldil sends: "Never did He make two things the same; never did he utter one word twice. After earths, not better earths but beasts; after beasts, not better beasts but spirits. After a falling, not a recovery but a new creation. Out of the new creation, not a third but the mode of change itself is changed for ever. Blessed is He!" (*P,* 146–47).

Schwartz does not suggest that this vision of continuous development in the created universe has implications in Lewis's mind for the very being of the Creator, as existing in some kind of state of becoming. Lewis clearly opposes Bergson's view that God is to be identified with the life force, as a creative spirit that realizes itself progressively in the natural order. However, picking up my suggestion that there is an imaginative effect when the omnipresent center merges with the cosmic dance, we might say this is intensified when the dance itself is a continual process of becoming. The God who indwells a creation that is in a perpetual flux is even more likely to be a God who is mobile, not static, a God who joins the dance, or, rather, leads it onward.

But there may be another influence on Lewis that has not, I think, been noticed hitherto. We know that Lewis read all the novels of his friend Charles Williams, and among them there is *The Greater Trumps* (1932), which is entirely structured by the idea of the cosmic dance. The gypsy family of Henry Lee has guarded through many ages a set of a hundred golden figures that move in a perpetual and complex dance, reflecting the dance of the cosmos and all the movements of people and nations in the world. Henry believes that if the golden figures can be reunited with a pack of ancient tarot cards carrying the same images, he will be able to control space and time. The tarot cards are inherited by Mr. Coningsby, the father of his fiancée, Nancy, and the plot of the book consists of Henry's attempt to get possession of the cards, even if he must kill the obstinate Coningsby to do so. I will not relate the whole plot, but suffice it to say that the cards and figures spin out of Henry's control and threaten to bring an apocalyptic end to the world, a disaster averted only by the mystery of love.

In a chapter called "The Dance in the World," Henry explains the cosmic dance to Nancy: "Imagine that everything which exists takes part in the movement of a great dance—everything, the electrons, all growing and decaying things, all that seems alive and doesn't seem alive, men and beasts, trees and stones, everything that changes, and there is nothing anywhere that does not change. That change—that's what we know of the immortal dance; the law in the nature of things—that's the measure of the dance, why one thing changes swiftly and another slowly." As the figures dance, and unite with the cards, Nancy and Henry have a vision of the world, and see into the movements of peoples, armies, and civilizations: "All earth had been gathered up: this was the truth of earth. The dance went on in the void; only even there she saw in the centre the motionless Fool, and about him in a circle the Juggler ran, forever tossing his balls."[30]

This scene focuses on two key images in the tarot pack and among the golden figures. In the whirling, perpetual dance there is one figure, standing right in the center, who appears to remain unmoving—the Fool; there is, says Henry, an unfathomable mystery about this figure. The Fool is the number zero in the tarot pack, and so is the one who cannot be counted and numbered. By contrast, the most mobile figure is the Juggler, dancing and tossing his balls. Without delving into more esoteric lore, it is clear that the Juggler is the *Primum Mobile* of medieval cosmology, the first moved reality moving the other spheres (balls), and the Fool represents God, or at least the divine principle, who remains unmoving but who is the cause of movement in everything. Now, however, Williams overturns this world-picture. Nancy's aunt Sybil, a kind of prophetess, has a moment of spiritual insight as she looks at the golden figures dancing: she sees the Fool move. She says, "Surely that's it [the Fool], dancing with the rest; it seems as if it were always arranging itself in some place that was empty for it. . . ." Henry says in wonderment, "No one has ever seen it move. But . . . She saw it completing the measures, fulfilling the dance." Later, in the storm that has been loosed by the tarot cards which have slipped from Henry's hand, she cries: "'They say he doesn't move. . . . but I saw him move . . . and there's no figure anywhere in heaven or earth that can slip from that partner. They are all his for ever.' 'Do you think the Tarots can ever escape while the Fool is there to hold them?' 'Never mind the storm; it's nothing; it's under the feet of the Fool.'" Earlier, looking at the "dance in the world," Nancy herself sees the Fool and the Juggler moving toward each other and embracing each other. At the climax of the book, it is the Fool who comes to rescue Nancy, who is to be the new Eve, coming at the call of love: "He [the Fool] had come from all sides at once, yet he was but one. All-reconciling and perfect, he was there."[31]

Did Williams put the germ of an idea in Lewis's mind that the One who is at the center of the dance actually moves himself, despite the (Neoplatonist) tradition that insists he is the Unmoved Mover? "They say he doesn't move . . . but I saw him move," says Sybil.[32] If he is love, the vulnerable love of a Fool, then he must participate in the dance. Williams and Bergson are two possible influences, but Lewis has made the decisive step himself.

THE CENTER BEGETS ITSELF

The hymn that begins the Great Dance gives another clue to Lewis's thought about the moving center. We hear the voices say, "All things are by Him and for Him. He utters Himself also for his own delight and sees that He is good. He is his own begotten and what proceeds from Him is Himself. Blessed be He!" (*P,* 250–51). This clearly refers to the Christian doctrine of the eternal generation of the Son from the Father, and in various places Lewis repeats the metaphors for this generation formulated by Church Fathers such as Athanasius—the outshining of light from a lamp, the radiating of heat from a fire, or the speaking of a word from the mind. To these, however, Lewis adds the image of the dance. In *Perelandra,* the dance is only implicitly an image for divine generation, the association being made through the context of the opening hymn of praise, but the link is made explicitly elsewhere. In *The Problem of Pain* (1940), Lewis urges us not to hold on to our self, but to give it up, as players in a game pass on the ball to other players, a game that God plays with God's own self:

> When [the ball] flies to and fro among the players too swift for the eye to follow, and the great Master himself leads the revelry, giving Himself eternally to his creatures in the generation, and back to Himself in the sacrifice, of the Word, then indeed the eternal dance 'makes heaven drowsy with the harmony.' All pains and pleasures we have known on earth are early intimations in the movements of that dance: but the dance itself is strictly incomparable with the sufferings of the present time. As we draw nearer to its uncreated rhythm, pain and pleasure sink almost out of sight, There is joy in the dance, but it does not exist for the sake of joy. It does not even exist for the sake of good, or of love. It [i.e. the dance] is Love Himself, and Good Himself.[33]

Here the ball game played by the *Primum Mobile,* portrayed as the young girl in the picture to which Lewis refers,[34] or as the Juggler (tossing the spheres) in Williams's novel, is played by God himself. The cosmic dance is God's dance, and the rhythm is "uncreated"; indeed, the dance is Love and so is God. The primal dance is the going out of the Son from the Father "in the generation," and his return to the Father in obedient sacrifice.

In medieval theology, efforts were made to reconcile what appears to be divine movement in the eternal generation of the Son (and the perichoresis of the Trinity) with the cosmological belief that that the center of all things is still and motionless. In Thomas Aquinas, the movement of the Son out from, and back to, the Father is explained as being entirely compatible with immobility; like the emission of light from the sun, or emanation of thought from the mind, says Thomas, there is a kind of motion (*kinesis*), but this is identical with rest (*stasis*), echoed in the stability to which—as we have seen—Bonaventure refers us. Thomas Aquinas writes that "The conception and birth of an intelligible word. . . . involves neither motion nor succession."[35] While dynamic images of light from the sun and the word from the mind might be accommodated to *stasis* in this paradoxical way, it is clear that the image of a dance cannot, and so Lewis's own image affirms the movement of God is self-begetting, without equivocation, in a way that would be disturbing to medieval cosmology.

THE MOVING CENTER AND THEODICY

The primordial dance between the Father and the Son is the basis for the dance of creation, all created beings emanating from God and returning to God according to the pattern of the Son. This picture enables Lewis to include the evil and suffering of the world within the dance: they disturb its measures but finally they are overcome and transformed within its movement. Earlier, in *The Problem of Pain*, Lewis had appealed to the image of the dance: "God saw the crucifixion in the act of creating the first nebula. The world is a *dance* in which good, descending from God, is disturbed by evil arising from the creatures, and the resulting conflict is resolved by God's own assumption of the suffering nature which evil produces" (*PP*, 72). So in the Great Dance of Perelandra, we hear the voices say, "In the Fallen World He prepared for Himself a body and was united with the Dust and made it glorious for ever . . . the fountain that sprang with mingled blood and life in the Dark World, flows here with life only" (*P*, 248). Lewis's approach to the problem of evil at this time was a mixture of several rational elements: to the so-called "free will defence" (*PP*, 57), he added an assertion of the instrumental nature of suffering (pain is God's "megaphone" to rouse a deaf world [*PP*, 81]) and the relativizing of suffering by final joy (*PP*, 132). There are intellectual problems with all these elements, but I believe that Phillip Tallon is right to emphasize that Lewis's theodicy is finally not a rational argument but an *aesthetic* appeal to the universe as a work of art; the image of the dance draws us away from merely *intellectual* argument into seeing that God has the power to incorporate change, even rebellion and sin, into a beautiful whole.[36]

This will only convince by participation in it, by joining in the measures of the dance, an art form that includes persons.

Nor is this a wholeness of beauty that suppresses the individual and the particular, as in a Hegelian synthesis. The image of the dance has room to honor all participants rather than subjecting them to the necessity of a process. In the hymn of praise, every world and its inhabitants are given significance. Echoing the speech of God in Job 38–39, the place of things in creation is not to be measured by whether they seem relevant to the development of the human spirit. God asks Job, "Where were you when I laid the foundations of the earth [and] shut in the sea with doors?" (Job 38:4–8), and the voices here proclaim that "the waters you have not floated on, the fruit you have not plucked, the caves into which you have not descended and the fire through which your bodies cannot pass, do not wait for you to put on perfection" (*P,* 248).

In the vision that follows, the dance appears to Ransom as an intertwining of "many cords or bands of light, leaping over and under one another and mutually embraced in arabesques and flower-like subtleties. Each figure as he looked at it became the master-figure of focus of the whole spectacle" (*P,* 251). These bands of light, which weave together, are all "individual entities" (*P,* 252). Ransom reflects, "Some of the thinner and more delicate cords were beings that we call short-lived: flowers and insects, a fruit or a storm of rain, and once (he thought) a wave of the sea. Others were such things as we also think lasting: crystals, rivers, mountains, or even stars" (*P,* 252). More luminous bands, flashing with color, were "the lines of personal beings, different from one another in splendour" (*P,* 252). Not all the cords were individual beings—some were "universal truths or universal qualities" (*P,* 252). But the point is this: the ribbons of light were to be contrasted with what Lewis calls "mere generalities" (*P,* 252), or "the secular generalities of which history tells—nations, institutions, climates of opinion, civilizations, arts, sciences and the like" (*P,* 252). The generalities, beloved of Hegelians, were merely tiny atoms of momentary brightness that appeared where the cords intersected—"ephemeral coruscations that piped their short song and vanished" (*P,* 252). Lewis's portrayal of the dance, this ever-moving work of art, can convince us that everything can be included in God's generous love in a way that an abstract theodicy cannot.

The Freedom of the Dance

This reflection brings us to the way that the Great Dance embodies the themes of the novel. In this story of an unfallen world, and the temptation offered to its Eve, Lewis is working out a problem that perplexed Augustine in his account of the human Fall. Granted that humans are created with the freedom to disobey God, why would a person created in the bliss of communion with God *want* to fall away at all? Why would created beings *want* to turn away from the Good if they lived in unrestricted relation to the Good? Augustine himself found this to be an insoluble question that simply confirmed the nature of evil as "non-being" and its origin as a mystery.[37] The same question has led some modern theologians to doubt whether it is at all coherent to think, as Augustine does, of a strict sequence of perfection followed by a fall at one point in time.[38] Lewis, however, wants to keep a primordial paradise and comes up with his own solution: an unfallen being, enjoying full communion with God, could be persuaded to disobey only if she believed that this was in the service of a greater Good.

The Enemy therefore puts it to the Lady that Maleldil really wants her to disobey his commandment not to spend the night on the fixed land. Such disobedience is the only way to growth and maturity, and God *wants* the Lady to develop in knowledge and experience. The Good of obedience, the Enemy urges, is outweighed by the Good of growth, of "growing older" in wisdom. We know, as the Lady knows intuitively, that this is nonsense. Nothing can be better, more productive of joy, than obedience to Maleldil. In his study of Milton's *Paradise Lost*, Lewis had used the image of the dance precisely to express the joy of obedience to God and the freedom this creates: "Discipline, while the world is yet unfallen, exists for the sake of what seems its very opposite—for freedom, almost for extravagance. The pattern hidden deep in the dance, hidden so deep that shallow spectators cannot see it, alone gives beauty to the wild, free gestures that fill it. . . . Without sin, the universe is a Solemn Game: and there is no good game without rules."[39] Like a planet in the cosmic dance, the happy soul is a "wandering star" (*PPL*, 80), and yet in that very wandering she follows the invariable patterns of the dance. Lewis, however, moves just a little beyond the sheer paradox that obedience *is* perfect freedom, to hint that God might use this freedom to shape the very patterns of the dance itself. This is where the reversal of the tradition of the unmoving center is finally leading us. There is just a clue that through obedience we share in the creativity of God.

Here Lewis's mood is very different from that of Williams, who finds the dance to be a symbol of cosmic necessity. Henry Lee tells Nancy that the dance "is always perfect because it can't be anything else. It knows nothing of joy or grief. . . . If you cry, it's because the measure will have it so; if you laugh, it's because some gayer step *demands* it."[40] It is because of this necessity that Henry thinks he can control the world around him; if only he can read the movements, he can exploit them in his own actions.

Lewis takes freedom more seriously. When Ransom first meets the Green Lady, something he says gives her a new perception. She had thought that Maleldil simply presented her with one good thing after another, one wave rolling in after another, but now she sees that she plays her own part. "I thought that I was carried in the will of Him I love," she exclaims, "but now I see that I walk with it. . . . One's own self to be walking from one good to another, walking beside Him as Himself may walk. . . . I thought we went along paths—but it seems there are no paths. The going itself is the path" (*P,* 78). As well as confirming that the center of all things does indeed move, *walking* in and through the world, she perceives that there are no preordained paths: the obedient person creates them with God in the very going. After the vision of the dance, the King of Perelandra predicts that this freedom can only increase as beings grow and develop: "I believe the waves of time will often change for us henceforward. We are coming to have our own choice whether we shall be above them and see many waves together or whether we shall reach them one by one as we used to" (*P,* 254).

This perception illuminates what seems an obscure ending to the hymn of praise: "If we never meet the dark, and the road that leads nowhither, and the question to which no answer is imaginable, we should have in our minds no likeness of the Abyss of the Father, into which if a creature drop down his thoughts for ever he shall hear no echo return to him." It is just because the paths of the dance are not a predetermined necessity that we experience a need for courage in walking out into the dark.[41]

So it is that "the going itself is the path." This is surely the point of the vision of the Great Dance, where the ribbons or cords of light, the patterns of the dance, *are* the myriad created things themselves. *They* are the pattern, just as Love *is* the Dance.

NOTES

1. Teresa Hooper makes an important contrast between the select "inner ring" and the universal dance in "Playing by the Rules: Kipling's 'Great Game' vs. 'the Great Dance' in C. S. Lewis's Space Trilogy," *Mythlore* 25, no. 1–2 (Sept. 2006): 105–26.

2. C. S. Lewis, *P* (London: Bodley Head, 1967), 244.

3. Bonaventure, *Itinerarium Mentis In Deum* V.8; Alan of Lille, *Regulae de Sacra Theologia*, rule 7. Jaime Vidal draws attention to Bonaventure in "The Ubiquitous Center in Bonaventure and Lewis," but his argument is quite different from mine. Jaime Vidal, "The Ubiquitous Center in Bonaventure and Lewis: With Application to the Great Dance on Perelandra," *CSL: Bulletin of the New York C. S. Lewis Society* 6, no. 5 (Mar. 1975), 1–6.

4. Bonaventure, *Itinerarium Mentis In Deum* V.8.

5. Aristotle, *Physics* 8.10; Aristotle, *Metaphysics* 12.6–7.

6. Plotinus, *Enneads* V.2.1–2. Plotinus differs from Aristotle in that the unmoved Absolute Good or the One is not itself an intelligence; the principle of mind (*nous*) is an emanation from the Good (*Enneads* V.6.1–5).

7. Plotinus, *Enneads* II.2.1–2: "The centre is a point of rest . . . the Soul exists in revolution around God to whom it clings in love."

8. C. S. Lewis, *DI* (Cambridge, UK: Cambridge Univ. Press, 1964), 113; emphasis added.

9. Bonaventure, *Itinerarium* V.8, citing Boethius, *De Consolatione Philosophiae* III. 9 (poem).

10. Sanford Schwartz, "Paradise Reframed: Lewis, Bergson, and Changing Times on Perelandra," *Christianity and Literature* 51, no. 4 (Summer 2002): 592.

11. See, for example, Roland M. Kawano, "C. S. Lewis and the Great Dance," *Christianity and Literature* 26, no. 1 (1976), 28.

12. The *Primum Mobile* in Ptolemaic astronomy is the outermost concentric sphere of the universe: see Dante, *Paradiso* 27.97–148. Milton refers to the "First-moved" in *Paradise Lost*, 3.482.

13. Ibid. The reference is to Jean Seznec, *The Survival of the Pagan Gods. Mythological Tradition and its Place in Renaissance Humanism and Art*, trans. B. F. Sessions (New York: Pantheon, 1953), 80.

14. Cf. T. S. Eliot, "the still point of the turning world," in Eliot, "Burnt Norton" IV, "Four Quartets," in *The Complete Poems and Plays of T. S. Eliot* (London: Faber and Faber, 1969), 185.

15. Pseudo-Dionysius, *The Celestial Hierarchy*, 7.4 (209D-212B); cf. 7.1 (205B-C).

16. Dante, *Paradiso* 28.121–29. Dante does not explicitly mention a dance, however, only "whirling."

17. C. S. Lewis, *Beyond Personality*, in his *MC*, 138–39. I elaborate on Lewis's concept of the Trinity in "On Theology," in *The Cambridge Companion to C. S.*

Lewis, ed. Robert McSwain and Michael Ward (Cambridge, UK: Cambridge Univ. Press, 2010), 90–95, 99–101.

18. For more on participation, see C. S. Lewis's "Meditation in a Toolshed" (1945), in his *U*, 171–74, where he distinguishes between "looking at" and "looking along" things, the latter being a matter of "stepping inside."

19. See, for example, William J. Hill, *The Three-Personed God: The Trinity as a Mystery of Salvation* (Washington, D.C.: Catholic Univ. of America Press, 1982), 272; Catherine M. LaCugna, *God For Us: The Trinity and Christian Life* (San Francisco, Calif.: HarperCollins, 1991), 271; Elizabeth Johnson, *She Who Is: The Mystery of God in Feminist Theological Discourse* (New York: Crossroad, 1993), 220–21; Paul S. Fiddes, *Participating in God: A Pastoral Doctrine of the Trinity* (London: Darton, Longman, & Todd, 2000), 72–81.

20. Plotinus, *Enneads* 4.4.33.

21. Basil, *Hom.* in *Hexaëmeron* 4.

22. Dante, *Paradiso* 10.76–91.

23. John Davies, *Orchestra; or, A Poem of Dancing* (London: Chatto and Windus, 1947), verse 12.

24. G. R. S. Mead, trans. and ed., *The Hymn of Jesus* (London: Theosophical Publishing Society, 1907), 37; set to music by Gustav Holst.

25. "Tomorrow Shall Be my Dancing Day," verse.2, apparently first printed in *Christmas Carols Ancient and Modern*, ed. William B. Sandys (London: Richard Beckley, 1833), 110.

26. Schwartz, "Paradise Reframed," 574.

27. Ibid., 569–70, 580–81. See also Sanford Schwartz, *C. S. Lewis on the Final Frontier: Science and the Supernatural in the Space Trilogy* (New York: Oxford Univ. Press, 2009), 55–73.

28. On Malacandra, the hrossa had already tried to teach Ransom that pleasures in love and poetry should be remembered rather than replicated; see C. S. Lewis, *OSP* (London: Bodley Head, 1967), 82–83.

29. C. S. Lewis, *LWW* (London: Collins, 1974), 39–41.

30. Charles Williams, *The Greater Trumps* (London: Faber & Faber, 1964 [1932]), 94, 102.

31. Williams, *Greater Trumps*, 74, 86, 139–40, 103, 228.

32. Ibid., 139.

33. C. S. Lewis, *PP* (London: Geoffrey Bles, 1940), 141. There are many echoes of these final pages of *The Problem of Pain* in the Great Dance of Perelandra.

34. See note 13 above.

35. Thomas Aquinas, *Summa Contra Gentiles* 4, 11, n. 18. Similarly, Maximus the Confessor ascribes to the Spirit a "rest that is eternally in motion and constant motion that is at rest" (*Quaestiones ad Thalassium* PG90, 760A). While Gregory of Nyssa writes that "rest and motion are identical," he refers this not to God but to the soul that God has invited into his infinity (*De Vita Moysis* PG 44.405 BD). Earlier, Plotinus had ascribed "simultaneous rest and motion" to the *nous*, circling

in itself and returning to itself (*Enneads* II.3), but not to "the One," which remains motionless.

36. Philip Tallon, "Evil and the Cosmic Dance: C. S. Lewis and Beauty's Place in Theodicy," in *C. S. Lewis as Philosopher: Truth, Goodness and Beauty*, ed. David Baggett, Gary R. Habermas, and Jerry L. Walls (Downers Grove, Ill.: InterVarsity Press, 2008), 208–10.

37. Augustine, *De Civitate Dei*, 12.7, 14.13.

38. See, for example, Friedrich Schleiermacher, *The Christian Faith*, trans. H. R. Mackintosh and J. S. Stewart (Edinburgh: T. & T. Clark, 1928) 295; John Hick, *Evil and the God of Love* (London: Fontana, Collins, 1968), 75.

39. C. S. Lewis, *PPL* (London: Oxford Univ. Press, 1942), 79–80.

40. Williams, *Greater Trumps*, 95.

41. Exactly the same image of the abyss of the Father occurs in the passage on the dance in *The Problem of Pain*, 141–42. Perhaps there is an echo of Jacob Boehme, for whom the Abyss in God is both Non-Being and Absolute Freedom; see *De Signatura Rerum* 2: 7–10; Lewis writes of reading chapter 2 of *De Signatura Rerum* in 1930, urging "we must worry it out." C. S. Lewis, *CL.* III (London: HarperCollins, 2006), 1515.

Perelandra in Its Own Time

A Modern View of the Space Trilogy

SANFORD SCHWARTZ

In the first two volumes of the Space Trilogy, *Out of the Silent Planet* (1938) and *Perelandra* (1943), C. S. Lewis presents his readers with a clear line of continuity and development as they proceed from one novel to the next. The continuity rests primarily on the conflict between the Christian protagonist, Elwin Ransom, and his two ruthless foes—the physicist Weston and the venture capitalist Devine—who are introduced in *Out of the Silent Planet* and who resurface in the two sequels—Weston in *Perelandra* and Devine (as Lord Feverstone) in *That Hideous Strength* (1945). The sense of development is most apparent in the gradual transformation of the hero, who progresses from a confused captive to an anointed agent of divine redemption as he confronts the demonic powers that threaten the beneficent order of the created universe. Equally important, however, are the largely neglected changes that occur in Ransom's enemies and in the modern "evolutionary" or "developmental" model they explicitly represent.

In *Out of the Silent Planet,* Ransom's antagonists are associated with the popular "materialist" view of the evolutionary process—the infamous "struggle for existence"[1]—especially as it appears in H. G. Wells's portrayal of interplanetary invasion in *The War of the Worlds* and elsewhere. The two villains use the presumption of their own evolutionary superiority to justify the conquest, displacement, or outright extermination of other rational beings, whether they are members of other species, as they are on Malacandra (Mars), or "inferior" members of our own species here on Earth.[2] In *Perelandra,* Ransom once again encounters Weston, who has been converted to "biological philosophy" and now espouses the vision of perpetual cosmic progress as it appears in Henri Bergson's "creative evolution" and the British "emergent evolution" that followed in its wake. At first glance, the physicist's conversion may seem a distinction without a difference, since the encounter between Ransom and Weston (or rather, the Satanic Un-man who gradually takes possession of Weston's mind) rapidly descends, as it does in the first book, into a mortal conflict between Christian tradition and modern apostasy. Nevertheless, as readers of Lewis's "interstellar romances," we should not be too quick to shrug off the evil professor's newfound faith. In many of his other writings, Lewis discriminates carefully between the "materialist" (or "mechanistic") view of "orthodox Darwinism"[3] and the "organic" (or "vitalist") view of creative/emergent evolution, and though he is critical of each of these stances, he refuses to equate the one with the other. Moreover, the distinction between *Wellsianity* (his term) and *Bergsianity* (my term) plays a constitutive role in the Space Trilogy. As we shall see, certain features of Lewis's Malacandra suggest that this spiritually uncorrupted planet should be regarded as the "sublimation" or "taking up" of the Wellsian war between the species,[4] while the distinctive temporal dynamism of Perelandra may be considered a sanctified version of "creative evolution" itself. In line with his Augustinian view that "bad things are good things perverted,"[5] Lewis transforms first the mechanistic and then the vitalist views of evolution into pristine worlds that make their terrestrial counterparts appear as parodic distortions of unspoiled and divinely created originals. In this respect, the distinction between Wellsianity and Bergsianity illuminates not only the changing character of the evil powers in the two interstellar romances but also some of the most salient differences between the unfallen worlds that Lewis envisions on Mars and Venus before returning to Earth in the final volume of the series.

BERGSON AND LEWIS

To appreciate the difference between mechanistic and vitalist views of the evolutionary process, we must take a closer look at creative evolution and the function it served in early-twentieth-century culture. The term itself is associated specifically with the philosopher Henri Bergson, whose

Creative Evolution (1907) became one of the most influential books of the period.[6] Bergson's theory of evolution developed out of his pioneering reformulation of the concept of time, which upset the traditional priority of Being over Becoming and paved the way for the British movement of emergent evolution—expressed most notably in Samuel Alexander's *Space, Time and Deity* (1920) and C. Lloyd Morgan's *Emergent Evolution* (1923)—which modified the Darwinian paradigm to allow more room for novelty, discontinuity, and creative development in the evolutionary process. Bergson also laid the foundation for the subsequent explorations of temporal process that appeared in the later works of Alfred North Whitehead—*Science and the Modern World* (1925) and *Process and Reality* (1929)—and (though unacknowledged at the time) in the writings of the French existentialists of the thirties and forties. Moreover, as the ostensible middle way between materialist and religious points of view, Bergson's "vitalist" or "Life-Force philosophy" played a significant, if controversial, role in early-twentieth-century religious thought.[7] As we shall see, Lewis read Bergson with much enthusiasm in his early years, and even his more critical view of the philosopher after his midlife conversion to Christianity indicates some of the ways that *Perelandra* takes up Bergson's vision of creation as a process of continuous and innovative development.[8]

On the basis of his first two books, *Time and Free Will* (1889) and *Matter and Memory* (1896), Bergson established a significant reputation as a critic of positivism, demonstrating that the mechanistic procedures designed to explore the physical world are insufficient for the study of mental life. In contrast to association psychologists, whose picture of the mind as a collection of discrete impersonal "atoms" is modeled on the laws of physics, Bergson asserted that consciousness in "real duration" (*durée réelle*) is not a sequence of isolatable moments but rather a seamless continuity in a "constant state of becoming"—a process of continuous development in which each new moment is permeated by all that has come before it—and is therefore irreducible to the forms of explanation employed in the physical sciences. In an intellectual milieu still dominated by positivism, Bergson's early works appealed to many younger intellectuals, who flocked to his lectures and referred to him as the "liberator"—the philosopher who redeemed Western thought from the nineteenth century's "religion of science." Soon after the turn of the century, however, Bergson's thought began to develop along lines that would alienate many of his early admirers by extending the idea of real duration from the human mind to the natural universe itself. In *An Introduction to Metaphysics* (1903), Bergson maintained that absolute reality does not reside in a system of unchanging forms comprehended (or constituted) by the "intellect" but in the mobile flux given to us directly through "intuition." This "inversion of Platonism" offered a dramatic challenge to traditional ways of thought, and its implications became explicit several years later with the appearance of *Creative Evolution.*

In his wide-ranging and enormously influential magnum opus, Bergson simultaneously dismantles the Darwinian theory of evolution, which is based on the mechanistic explanations of the intellect, and proposes an alternative view in which real duration provides a model for the intuitive grasp of the perpetual movement of life itself. Tracing the problems of nineteenth-century positivism back to the origins of Western philosophy, Bergson claims that the rational intellect, by its very nature, reduces time to a function of space and that, as a consequence of this spatializing function, it treats the past and the future as calculable functions of the present. In other words, the intellect is an ingenious instrument for organizing and arranging the existing products of creation, but its inability to comprehend processes involving true novelty and unforeseeable change account not only for the problems of traditional metaphysics but also for the failure of modern scientific theories of evolution. In place of the latter, Bergson postulates the existence of a creative spiritual impetus, the *élan vital,* which spontaneously produces novel forms of life. Just as the human mind develops continuously in "real duration," the natural universe is impelled by a "vital impetus" that perpetually raises creation to new and previously unpredictable levels of development.

Creative Evolution was a huge popular success, and its author soon became an international celebrity. The basis of Bergson's remarkable appeal lay not simply in his critique of positivism but in his synthesis of opposing points of view. Under his spell, the presumably unbridgeable gap between religious and naturalistic viewpoints appeared to dissolve into mere illusion. Bergson achieved this feat by simultaneously spiritualizing the biological and naturalizing the spiritual realms. After reading his book, one could believe that the Darwinian model is essentially a consequence of the mechanistic nature of the intellect, and that the *élan vital* makes more sense of the entire evolutionary process. One could also discard the traditional metaphysical conception of God as a product of the intellect, which leads us to identify reality with stasis rather than dynamic process, and proceed to reenvision the Divine as an immanent creative spirit that realizes itself in the progressive development of the natural order. As it turned out, this middle way between the spiritual and the material did achieve a considerable—if momentary—following, but as a means of reconciling opposing points of view it was treated as a suspicious compromise by many on both sides of the ideological spectrum. Bergson's Catholic followers, such as Jacques Maritain and Charles Péguy, continued to applaud his distinction between the mechanistic realm of matter and the vital realm of animate existence, but at the same time they condemned him for collapsing the essential distinction between the vital and the religious realms by reducing the divine to an immanent life force.[9] Hence the Bergsonian synthesis proved to be an unstable compound, especially as the cultural climate began to change over the course of World War I; by the time the war was over, the ethos that could support the notion of an immanent spiritual impetus had seriously eroded. While the distinction between mechanistic and vital processes continued to play a significant role in postwar thought, the extraordinary vogue of Bergsonism began its steady decline.

Ironically, C. S. Lewis's interest in Bergson began while he was recovering from battlefront wounds in 1918, and the young scholar continued to read Bergson intermittently in the years that followed.[10] As might be expected, after his conversion in the early thirties Lewis assumed the more critical stance of Maritain and Péguy, affirming Bergson's separation of the mechanistic and vital realms but rejecting his virtual equation of the vital and the spiritual. According to the Christian Lewis, creative evolution is a "modern form of nature religion."[11] Its distinctive appeal lies in its "in-between view," which promises to deliver us from the "material" while diluting the "religious" into an emotionally uplifting but undemanding sense of "striving" or "purposiveness" in the natural universe (*MC*, 34–35). Nevertheless, even as he dissects the dangers and temptations of "Life-Force philosophy," Lewis never reduces Bergsianity to mere Wellsianity. In one of his classic accounts of the latter, he maintains that "the Bergsonian critique of orthodox Darwinism is not easy to answer."[12] He also treats Bergson himself with considerable respect, customarily distinguishing the philosopher's own works from the various popularizations of his ideas by George Bernard Shaw and others. In his autobiography, *Surprised by Joy* (1956), Lewis is quite open in his praise as he recalls his initial response to Bergson in 1918:

The other momentous experience was that of reading Bergson in a Convalescent Camp on Salisbury Plain. . . . [It also] had a revolutionary effect on my emotional outlook. Hitherto my whole bent had been toward things pale, remote, and evanescent; the water-color world of Morris, the leafy recesses of Malory, the twilight of Yeats. The word "life" had for me pretty much the same associations it had for Shelley in *The Triumph of Life*. I would not have understood what Goethe meant by *des Lebens goldnes Baum*. Bergson showed me. He did not abolish my old loves, but he gave me a new one. From him I first learned to relish energy, fertility, and urgency; the resource, the triumphs, and even the insolence, of things that grow. I became capable of appreciating artists who would, I believe, have meant nothing to me before; all the resonant, dogmatic, flaming, unanswerable people like Beethoven, Titian (in his mythological pictures), Goethe, Dunbar, Pindar, Christopher Wren, and the more exultant Psalms. (*SBJ*, 198)

For the young agnostic caught between a dreamy late Romanticism and the horror of the trenches, Bergson's way of infusing nature with spirit appears to have worked like a charm. In his later life Lewis may have become more critical of Bergson, but he respected the difference between the mechanistic and vitalist views of the evolutionary process. In the Space Trilogy, this distinction becomes crucial as we proceed from Ransom's first adventure in *Out of the Silent Planet* to his new expedition in *Perelandra*. More importantly, this distinction is evident not just in the villain's dubious awakening to the *élan vital* but in the uncorrupted worlds that Lewis constructs on Mars and Venus. Indeed, the new Eden on Perelandra may be regarded as Lewis's own paean to "the resource, the triumphs, and even the insolence, of things that grow"—a celebration of the vital realm that reaches its highest expression in the "*animal rationale*" (*P*, 178) who presides over the rest of creation. The Adversary may preach the gospel of creative or emergent evolution, but Lewis designs his own version of creative evolution by endowing his imaginary world with a principle of dynamic change in which even the evolutionary lapses, including the spiritual catastrophe that has overtaken our own fallen planet, are transfigured into something new and more marvelous by the redeeming act of God.

WELLS ON MARS, BERGSON ON VENUS

It is well known that Lewis endows his other worlds on Mars and Venus with attributes drawn from the medieval model of the cosmos—the "heavens which declared the glory"[13]—and populates them with unfallen rational creatures free from the fears and temptations that plague our own wayward species. Therefore it may seem surprising that these imaginary planets derive some of their most salient features from the same modern "evolutionary model" espoused by the terrestrial invaders. Seen from this perspective, each of the two unspoiled worlds with which Ransom is associated appears not as the polar opposite but the "beatific" transfiguration of the specific phase of the evolutionary model to which it stands opposed. In *Out of the Silent Planet,* the peace and harmony existing among Malacandra's three rational species may be seen as the "sublimation," or "working-up" (*RP,* 112) into a first principle, of Wells's Darwinian vision of evolution as a relentless struggle for existence. Similarly, Maleldil's creation of Perelandra's fluid and ever-progressing paradise may be regarded as the "up-grading" of Bergson's hospitable and temporally dynamic vision of cosmic development (*RP,* 116). Moreover, as a consequence of this artistic strategy, the two naturalistic theories of evolution—Wellsian and Bergsonian—are transformed into parodic distortions of the unfallen worlds for which they provided the imaginative impetus—that is, *Out of the Silent* provides a vision of interspecies harmony in relation to which the Wellsian struggle for existence appears as the corrupted version of an archetypal original, while *Perelandra* offers a distinctive paradisal vision that reduces Bergson's creative evolution to a degraded form of the authentic temporal dynamism with which Maleldil has endowed his new creation on Venus.[14]

In *Out of the Silent Planet,* Weston has not yet been converted to Bergson's "biological philosophy." His self-defined mission is simply to perpetuate his race by extending the Darwinian struggle for existence from our world to other sectors of the universe. Hence it is no accident that Lewis creates a Martian cosmopolis in which reason transcends biological differences, a civilization comprising three rational species—each with its own distinctive anatomy and temperament—that live separately but peacefully in a divinely ordered universe. Lewis's Malacandrans know nothing of the evolutionary struggle on our own planet, but once Ransom arrives on Mars his obsessive concern with the order of the species—their origins, development, and modes of relationship—indicates that Lewis is not only transporting us from a fallen to an uncontaminated world but also "taking up" the Wellsian view of "Nature, red in tooth and claw" into a cosmic vision in which the various species are bound together in universal brotherhood.[15] Significantly, the Malacandrans have not been immune to the natural perils that plague our own terrestrial existence. As a result of an ancient invasion by the fallen archangel who still reigns over the Earth, they have adapted to environmental change and learned to compensate for the irreparable physical damage to the surface of their planet. In the process they have also acquired the discipline and courage to overcome the insecurity—and above all the fear of death—that impels the mistrust and violence of life on our own "silent" planet. Moreover, at least one of their rational species exercises these martial virtues in the ritual of the hunt, a form of "unfallen" violence that expresses the ancient kinship between rational and irrational creatures and enhances the joy of life through the very risk of death. In this respect, the imaginary world of Malacandra is a composite entity—an uncorrupted planet akin to our own visions of the terrestrial paradise, but also an "up-grading" of the evolutionary struggle for existence into an "original," or archetype that simultaneously transfigures the "biocentric" view of universal strife and parodies its one-sided character.

It may seem a long way from the Darwinian survival of the fittest to the interspecies unity of Malacandra, but elsewhere in his writings Lewis shows us that it is not far-fetched to consider the creation on Mars as a transfiguration of the terrestrial condition of evolutionary strife. In his prose essays Lewis acknowledges the competitive brutality of the natural order, but he also maintains that in light of the Christian doctrine of creation, the undeniable "cruelty and wastefulness" of nature as we know it "may yet be derived from a principle which is good and fair, may indeed be a depraved and blurred copy of it—the pathological form which it would take in a *spoiled* Nature" (*M*, 156).[16] In the same way, Lewis's Malacandra embodies the transfiguration of "spoiled Nature"—that is, Nature as it appears in the materialist account of the evolutionary process—into its originary "principle"; or, seen from the opposite direction, the creation on Mars may be regarded as the archetype of which our own "*spoiled* Nature"—the "cruelty and wastefulness" of the struggle for existence—is the "depraved and blurred copy" (*M*, 156). Lewis's formulation descends from the venerable tradition of Neoplatonic thought, but to conceive the interspecies unity on Mars as the archetype of our own strife-torn planet takes us closer to some of Lewis's demonstrably modern concerns. Far from simply turning back the clock to a premodern conception of the heavens, Lewis's transfiguration of Wells's evolutionary naturalism capitalizes upon his predecessor's use of interplanetary conflict to explore the spiritual affliction at the source of our troubled relations with other members of our own species as well as with the other creatures with whom we share the Earth. If nothing else, Lewis is addressing the urgent issues of his own moment. The peace and equality shared by the three Martian species, who live apart but never seek to subordinate one another, underscore the opposite conditions here on Earth—the propensity of its single rational species to split into factions that regard each other as inherently alien or inferior, or even as creatures of a different species—an age-old affliction of our self-divided species that had been raised to a boiling point by the virulent nationalism and racism of the 1930s.[17]

Perelandra offers a more readily discernable example of the "taking up" of the evolutionary model into an imagined archetype. If *Out of the Silent Planet* at once rejects and raises up Wells's "orthodox Darwinism," *Perelandra* simultaneously repudiates and "sublimates" Bergson's affirmative vision of evolutionary progress. In this second interplanetary struggle, Weston's shift from materialist "Wellsianity" to vitalist "creative evolution" is reflected in the dynamic (and remarkably Bergsonian) character of the new creation that Ransom discovers on Venus.[18] When Ransom first arrives on this newly minted world, he is as yet unaware that his role is to protect the new Eve from the demonically possessed Weston and his seductive new creed. What Ransom does discover at the outset of his adventure is that the created order on Perelandra is dramatically different from its terrestrial counterpart. In a striking departure from traditional views of the earthly paradise, Lewis presents the prelapsarian condition as a state of continuous flux, a "universe of shifting slopes" (*P,* 34), and he portrays its crowning achievement—its Adam and Eve—as dynamic creatures who are fast learners and seem to develop with every passing moment. Instead of an immutable condition that precedes the Fall into time and change, Lewis's new Eden is a world of perpetual movement in which the one prohibition—its Tree of the Knowledge of Good and Evil—is to avoid habitation of the "Fixed Land." This feature of the novel rarely receives the attention it deserves: when it is not simply taken for granted or chalked up as a clever conceit, it is attributed either to hints of an evolving Eden in Milton's *Paradise Lost* or to the "floating islands" that often appeared in extant scientific accounts of Venus's atmosphere.[19] These are significant sources, but the shift from Being to Becoming in Lewis's mobile paradise is so pronounced, and the psychological, spiritual, and cosmological implications of this "inversion of Platonism" explored in such exacting detail, that a more far-reaching alternative suggests itself— that the new world on Perelandra is not merely a reconstruction of the biblical conception of paradise, nor an extrapolation from "the discarded image" of medieval cosmology, but a sublimated and Christianized form of creative evolution itself. In fact, the Bergsonian stamp appears virtually everywhere in this perpetually evolving planet. It is evident not only in the continuous development of the untarnished Green Lady—the Eve of this new Eden—but also in the ceaseless novelty and progress of Maleldil's wondrous creativity: "Never did He make two things the same; never did He utter one word twice. After earths, not better earths but beasts; after beasts, not better beasts, but spirits. After a falling, not a recovery but a new creation. Out of the new creation, not a third but the mode of change itself is changed for ever. Blessed is He!" (P, 184). Of course this celebration of the transcendent Creator involves a significant departure from Bergson. Whereas the philosopher equates the divine with the immanent development of life itself (*élan vital*), Lewis attempts to raise Bergson's vision of perpetual development to a higher power, reversing his naturalization of the supernatural and reshaping his model of cosmic progress into a Christian vision of Becoming.

At first glance it seems strange, if not contradictory, to think of Lewis assembling his new Eden according to a blueprint provided by the enemy Himself. But such a view of *Perelandra* grows less perplexing if we consider Lewis's contemporaneous study of Milton, *A Preface to Paradise Lost* (1942). In this highly influential work, Lewis overturns William Blake's reading of Milton as "of the Devil's party without knowing it" by reducing Satan from an exalted tragic hero to a parody of the God against whom he has rebelled.[20] Invoking the Augustinian notion that evil has no substantial existence and is merely a defection from the Good, Lewis shows that Milton's fallen archangel should be regarded not as an authentic hero but as a warped imitation of his Creator. The same logic, which presupposes that God "has no opposite,"[21] may account for the otherwise baffling situation in *Perelandra*, where Lewis presents creative evolution as a dangerous distortion of the divinely ordained and beneficent temporal dynamism of his own imaginary paradise. Armed with Augustine's view that "what we call bad things are good things perverted" (*PPL*, 66), Lewis took the Platonic step of conceiving an "original," or an archetype, which "takes up" creative evolution to a higher level and simultaneously reduces it to a misshapen derivative. Put somewhat differently, just as Bergson transfigured a mechanistic theory of evolution still entangled in the static categories of traditional metaphysics into a new principle of Becoming, so Lewis transfigures Bergson's vitalistic naturalism, rejecting his reduction of the divine to an immanent creative impetus but reworking his radical reformulation of evolutionary theory into a Christian conception of continuous cosmic development.

THE STRANGE CASE OF *THAT HIDEOUS STRENGTH*

The first two novels of the Space Trilogy form a coherent set. In each instance the journey "into another dimension" involves the sublimation of one version of the modern evolutionary paradigm into its imagined archetype. But does the progression from the materialist view of *Out of the Silent Planet* to the organic view of *Perelandra* tell us anything about *That Hideous Strength,* which abandons interplanetary adventure in favor of the earthbound "spiritual shockers" of Charles Williams? In the finale to the series, Ransom remains on his own planet to battle Divine and his seemingly scientific institution—the National Institute of Co-ordinated Experiments (N.I.C.E.)—whose leaders are actually conspiring with de-monic powers to seize control of the evolutionary process and bring about the self-transformation of man into "God almighty . . . a being made by man—who will finally ascend to the throne of the universe. And rule for-ever."[22] As paradoxical as it seems, the modern developmental paradigm as it appears in *That Hideous Strength* is no longer tethered to its natural-istic moorings. As the titular allusion to the Tower of Babel suggests, the N.I.C.E. transports us beyond both the material (Wellsian) and the organic (Bergsonian) realms to the spiritual (Babelian) plane of the supernatural "New Man, who will not die, the artificial man, free from nature" (*THS,* 174). Strangely enough, as we progress through the trilogy we are also progressing to seemingly higher forms of the evolutionary model itself as it aspires to ascend, and in a sense return, to the transcendent heights of the religious worldview it had presumably left behind.[23]

If the concluding novel of the series sustains the progression from the material to the organic conceptions of evolution in the first two novels, can we find anything in the earthbound finale corresponding to the "up-grading" of the developmental model that takes place on the unfallen planets of the first two novels? Lewis has abandoned the literary form of the previous tales, but, in shifting to the "supernatural thrillers" of Charles Williams, he is turning to a fictional "formula" in which the process of imaginary transfiguration to an original informing "principle" plays a fundamental role.[24] Much has been made of Williams's study of magic and the occult, but the source of his fictional "formula" lies primarily in the blending of "the Probable and the Marvellous" (*OTOW,* 46) that began in Gothic romances of the eighteenth century. The Faustian nec-romancers of Williams's shockers are staples of the Gothic tradition, but Williams raises Gothic terror to a higher dimension, ingeniously using its revenants, doppelgangers, and other spectral resources to "haunt" his modern protagonists and restore the palpable presence of the divine Omnipotence—the "dreadful goodness"—that creates and sustains the ordinary world we inhabit.[25] Lewis follows Williams in this double use of the Gothic to portray the Faustian aspirations of the N.I.C.E. while simultaneously reaffirming (in a distinctive mixture of Arthurian and Gothic romance) a traditional conception of the supernatural.[26] As in the "working-up" of Wells on Mars and Bergson on Venus, the construction of a beatific "original" at the manor of St. Anne's, like the very form of the novel itself, retains many of the defining elements of the Gothic—above all, as Lewis puts it in a letter to Dorothy L. Sayers on December 6, 1945, its trademark "mixture of the realistic and the supernatural" (*CL* II, 682)—that ultimately reduce the hideous techno-magical power of the N.I.C.E. to a distorted Gothic double. In this respect, the last novel of the series employs a strategy virtually identical to that of its two predecessors.

The final volume of the Space Trilogy also completes a complex but co-herent pattern of confrontation and appropriation of the modern devel-opmental paradigm. It suggests that we should conceive the progression from the material to the spiritual both as a vertical hierarchy and as a horizontal sequence that proceeds from one novel to the next. Along the vertical axis we encounter the process of upwards transfiguration: each of the three novels "takes up" a distinctive version of the modern evolution-ary paradigm into a divinely sanctioned original, or first principle, which in turn reduces its modern target—ironically the very stuff out of which it has been conceived—into a parodic imitation. Along the horizontal axis we advance from the material (Wellsian) and organic (Bergsonian) to spiritual (Babelian) forms of the developmental model as it paradoxically reascends to the transcendent heights of the religious worldview it purports to supersede.[27] Fortunately, a familiar assumption underlies the relationship between vertical and horizontal axes. Like Arthur Lovejoy (in *The Great Chain of Being*, 1936) and many others, Lewis often represents the modern era in terms of a momentous historical change—the transposition of the source and center of Being from a transcendent God to the progressive development of man. As he describes it in *The Discarded Image* (1964), it is as if the multitiered medieval hierarchy (of which the three-level material/organic/spiritual hierarchy is the modern counterpart) has tumbled over on its side, and, as a result of this transformation, the traditional vertical relationship between lower and higher levels of Being has mutated into a horizontal progression from primitive to progressively more developed forms of life.[28] In the Space Trilogy, however, the modern developmental paradigm undergoes a series of self-transformations as we proceed throughout the series. As Lewis leads us from the material to the spiritual forms of this modern master myth, culminating in the techno-magical deification of man in *That Hideous Strength,* it becomes increasingly evident that he conceives evolutionary naturalism as merely a displaced and ultimately self-contradictory form of the multitiered cosmic hierarchy it has superseded. In the final analysis, the ostensibly horizontal model of perpetual progress begins to manifest (in progressively sinister fashion) the vertical character of its founding motivation and its ultimate aim, which lies in the ineradicable desire to transcend our finite condition and return to our spiritual homeland.

CONCLUSION

If Lewis designs his imaginary worlds by "taking up" the very things he is putting down, then we must reconsider the terms of engagement that have traditionally informed the interpretation of these novels. Ever since its publication, the Space Trilogy has been read primarily in terms of a sharply defined struggle between religious and naturalistic points of view, the first associated with the "discarded image" of premodern cosmology, the second with the modern "evolutionary model" that has supplanted it. There is much to support this approach, but it also obscures the more complex process of Lewis's world-building, which would be better served

by identifying the various subtypes of the evolutionary model and conceiving the conflict in each of these novels not simply as a clash between
two disparate and competing principles but as a relationship between an
archetype and its misshapen copy. In one sense, Lewis's creation of pristine
"originals" out of warped reproductions is merely a skillful adaptation of an
age-old polemical maneuver. As the critic Northrop Frye once described
it, the Augustinian strategy of transforming the ideological enemy into
a distorted derivative or demonic double reflects "the revolutionary and
dialectical element in Christian belief, which is constantly polarizing its
truth against the falsehoods of the heathen, but, like other revolutionary
doctrines, feels most secure when the dark side takes the form of a heresy
that closely resembles itself."[29] Lewis employs this conceptual maneuver
to reduce the opposition to a parodic imitation, but at the same time his
imagined archetypes bear witness to an irreducible element of receptivity
to the very "falsehoods" he is exposing. The imaginary Malacandra is not
only an unfallen planet that reflects the traditional conception of the heavens; it is also a transfiguration of the Darwinian struggle for existence into
the site of a modern exploration of the means through which we establish
the most basic distinctions between ourselves and other beings—and in
particular, the process that makes it possible for certain human beings to
relegate other members of their own kind to inferior or subhuman status.
Similarly, the evolving Eden on Perelandra, which is virtually inconceivable
in the absence of creative evolution, establishes the grounds of compat-
ibility between Christian orthodoxy and a distinctively modern conception
of time and temporal process. As for the conclusion of the series, scholars
have long regarded *That Hideous Strength* as a "Charles Williams novel
written by C. S. Lewis."[30] Nevertheless, the tendency to conceive the rival
powers in terms of a sheer antithesis between religious and naturalistic
worldviews, medieval romance and modern realism, covers up Lewis's ambitious attempt, inspired by Williams's own example, to employ the modern
Gothic mix of "the Probable and the Marvellous" (*OTOW,* 46) in a way
that does not simply revert to medieval romance but aspires to reactivate
the powers of enchantment (both demonic and divine) that have been cast
aside by the practitioners of modern realism. In this respect, Lewis's work
should be viewed not as a casual dismissal but as a searching exploration
of modern forms of thought and imaginative invention. As a result of this
adjustment of our optic, we may begin to see the Space Trilogy less as the
irreconcilable struggle between an old-fashioned Christian humanism

and a newfangled heresy than as the effort of a modern Christian writer to sustain and enrich the former through critical engagement with the latter.

Notes

1. H. G. Wells, *The War of the Worlds* (1898; Rockville, Md.: Arc Manor, 2008), 10.

2. In his prose essays, Lewis states repeatedly that his target is not the biological theory of evolution, which he regards as a "genuine scientific hypothesis" (C. S. Lewis, "The Funeral of a Great Myth," in his *CR* [Grand Rapids, Mich: Eerdmans, 1967], 83); it is the broader "developmental" paradigm that was well established by the time that *Origin of Species* appeared in 1859. In this respect, he regards Darwinism as the effect rather than the cause of the evolutionary model. In general, Lewis is less concerned with the prospect of subhuman ancestry than with the ideology that consigns other human beings to subhuman status or summons up an "evolutionary imperative" to legitimate the suspension of time-honored moral law.

3. See, for example, "Is Theology Poetry?" in C. S. Lewis, *WG* (New York: HarperCollins, 2001), 136.

4. C. S. Lewis, *RP* (San Diego, Calif.: Harcourt, 1958), 112, 116.

5. C. S. Lewis, *PPL* (London: Oxford Univ. Press, 1960), 66.

6. There are many expository and critical studies of Bergson, a fair portion of them from the period of his highest acclaim. Since the eclipse of his reputation in the middle third of the twentieth century, Bergson has been rehabilitated, primarily through the efforts of Gilles Deleuze, and he is again receiving attention as a seminal voice in modern philosophy.

7. See C. S. Lewis, *MC* (New York: Simon and Schuster, 1996), 34–35.

8. In *Perelandra*, Lewis uses the terms *creative evolution* and *emergent evolution* interchangeably, and elsewhere he equates them somewhat more dismissively with the "Life-Force philosophy" (*MC*, 34–35). The British fascination with a dynamic conception of nature is evident in the emergent evolutionists and in Whitehead, whom Lewis called "our greatest natural philosopher" (C. S. Lewis, *M* [New York: Simon and Schuster, 1996], 139). It also is evident in the more philosophical writings of well-known physicists such as Arthur Eddington, who included "Becoming" as a chapter in his influential book, *The Nature of the Physical World* (1928). Peter Bowler's formidable study, *Reconciling Science and Religion: The Debate in Early-Twentieth-Century Britain* (2001), situates emergent evolution and related developments in the context of the broader struggle between religious and scientific viewpoints in the first few decades of the century. Until quite recently, most accounts of French existentialism followed the lead of Sartre and his contemporaries in excluding Bergson from the canonical list of seminal precursors, which typically includes Kierkegaard, Nietzsche, Husserl, and Heidegger, among others. Contemporary scholars, such as Suzanne Guerlac

(*Literary Polemics: Bataille, Sartre, Valéry, Breton* [1997]), have addressed this problematic dismissal and confirm the formative influence of Bergson's reflections on the openness of time and its relationship to human freedom upon the French philosophers of the next generation.

9. Bergson continued to inspire many Catholic intellectuals, particularly those who believed that the Church must eventually come to terms with modernity. But by suggesting that the *élan vital* may be equated with God, Bergson had entered into a fatal collision course with Rome, which ultimately placed his works on the Index of Prohibited Books. The hierarchical division into three planes of being—the material (or "mechanistic"), the organic (or "vital"), and the spiritual (or "theological")—that arose largely in response to Bergson became a prominent feature of Catholic thought in early twentieth-century France. Students of Anglo-American modernism may be more familiar with its exposition in T. E. Hulme's posthumous *Speculations* (1924), which influenced T. S. Eliot and other like-minded intellectuals in the twenties and thirties. See note 11 on Lewis's use of the same three-tier hierarchy.

10. The main autobiographical account appears in *Surprised by Joy* (C. S. Lewis, *SBJ* [San Diego, Calif.: Harcourt, 1970], 198, 204, 211). In a letter to Arthur Greeves, written on June 19, 1920, Lewis mentions that he is reading Bergson (C. S. Lewis, *CL* I [San Francisco, Calif.: Harper, 2000], 494). His diary entry for September 17, 1923, states that he is "re-reading" *Creative Evolution.* The diary also records his reading in January 1924 of Bergson's *Mind-Energy* (*L'Énergie spirituelle*), a collection of essays published in 1919, and in February 1925 of *Matter and Memory* (C. S. Lewis, *AMR* [San Diego, Calif.: Harcourt, 1991], 269, 285, 349). Other references to Bergson appear throughout his later works.

11. C. S. Lewis, "The Grand Miracle," in his *GD* (New York: Simon and Schuster, 1996), 86.

12. Lewis, "Is Theology Poetry?" 136.

13. C. S. Lewis, *OSP* (New York: Scribner, 2003), 34

14. In his other writings, Lewis often employs the notion of "taking up" or extrapolating from a lower level to a higher one. The *locus classicus* may be found in his essay, "Transposition" (in his *WG*, 25–46), which assumes a three-level hierarchical ladder and focuses on, first, the modern tendency to reduce middle-level "human" phenomena (equivalent to Bergson's vital phenomena) to lower-level "material" causation, and, second, the correspondences that enable us to glimpse beyond the "human" to the "divine" level. The origins of this idea lie in Plato and the longstanding Neoplatonic tradition with which Lewis was intimately acquainted. But Lewis also drew on a fascinating modern source—the concept of the fourth dimension. In "Transposition" and elsewhere, Lewis turns to Edwin Abbott's immensely influential popularization, *Flatland: A Romance of Many Dimensions* (1884), as a model for projecting beyond the (three-dimensional) world we inhabit to a higher dimension—"God's dimension" (*MC,* 143)—to which the elements on the lower plane of our own existence may provide a certain degree of comprehension. On the sometimes startling results of the movement "upwards" and "downwards"

(occasionally conceived as "inwards" and "outwards"), see Lewis's account of the transposition process in the passage from our time-bound experience to our comprehension of the eternal (*MC*, 149; *M*, 187); in the imputed "sublimation" or "up-grading" of some of the all-too-human emotions expressed in the Psalms (*RP*, 112–16); in the transfiguration of our Old Nature into the New (Lewis, *M*, ch. 16); and (picking up on a cardinal point in the theological works of Charles Williams) in the Athanasian formulation of the Incarnation as proceeding "'not by the conversion of the godhead into flesh, but by taking of (the) manhood into God'" (*RP*, 116).

15. The infamous description of "Nature, red in tooth and claw" derives neither from Darwin nor from his followers but from Alfred Lord Tennyson, "In Memoriam A.H.H.," canto 56, line 15 (1850) in his *Selected Poems* (London: Penguin Classics, 2007), 135.

16. It is worth quoting the entire passage: "What the Christian story does is not to instate on the Divine level a cruelty and wastefulness which have already disgusted us on the Natural, but to show us in God's act, working neither cruelly nor wastefully, the same principle which is in Nature also, though down there it works sometimes in one way and sometimes in the other. It illuminates the Natural scene by suggesting that a principle which at first looked meaningless may yet be derived from a principle which is good and fair, may indeed be a depraved and blurred copy of it—the pathological form which it would take in a *spoiled* Nature" (*M*, 156).

17. I consider this aspect of the novel at some length in *C. S. Lewis on the Final Frontier: Science and the Supernatural in the Space Trilogy* (New York: Oxford Univ. Press, 2009), 19–52.

18. The difference between the "sublimation" of the material realm on Mars and the organic realm on Venus is evident in the physical descriptions of the two planets as well as in the celestial intelligences (Oyarsas) who preside over them. When the Oyarsas of Mars and Venus appear side by side at the end of *Perelandra*, they exhibit the traditional planetary distinction based on gender (masculine and feminine) and governing virtue (martial discipline and love), but they also bear the difference between the inorganic and the vital realms embodied by their respective planets: "The Oyarsa of Mars shone with cold and morning colours, a little metallic—pure, hard, and bracing. The Oyarsa of Venus glowed with a warm splendour, full of the suggestion of teeming vegetable life." C. S. Lewis, *P* (New York: Scribner, 2003), 171.

19. In a letter dated January 31, 1952, Lewis states that "the germ of *Perelandra* was simply the picture of the floating islands themselves, with no location, no story." C. S. Lewis, *CL* III (San Francisco, Calif.: Harper, 2007), 162. There is no reason to doubt that this image was the germ of the novel, but the picture of "floating islands" is insufficient to account for the extensive exploration of time and of the complexities of temporal experience that Lewis erected upon it. Equally insufficient are John Milton's suggestive remarks about paradise as a progressive state in which "bodies may at last turn all to spirit, / Improved by tract of time, and winged ascend / Ethereal, as we, or may at choice / Here or in heavenly para-

dises dwell" (Milton, *Paradise Lost,* ed. Scott Elledge [New York: W. W. Norton, 1993], 5.497–500). Lewis is heavily indebted to Milton, but it is arguable that for Lewis's readers the very focus upon his great predecessor has directed attention away from the modern elements in his fictive paradise. See Schwartz, *C. S. Lewis on the Final Frontier,* 53–90.

20. "The reason Milton wrote in fetters when he wrote of Angels & God, and at liberty when of Devils & Hell, is because he was a true Poet, and of the Devil's party without knowing it." William Blake, "The Marriage of Heaven and Hell" in *The Complete Poetry and Prose of William Blake,* ed. David V. Erdman, rev. ed. (New York: Anchor, 1997), 35. Another representative remark comes from Shelley: "Nothing can exceed the energy and magnificence of the character of Satan in 'Paradise Lost.' It is a mistake to suppose that he could ever have been intended for the popular personification of evil. . . . Milton's Devil as a moral being is so far superior to his God, as One who perseveres in some purposes which he has conceived to be excellent in spite of adversity and torture, is to One who in the cold security of undoubted triumph inflicts the most horrible revenge upon his enemy, not from any mistaken notion of inducing him to repent of a perseverance in enmity, but with the alleged design of exasperating him to deserve new torments." Percy Bysshe Shelley, *The Defence of Poetry* in *Shelley's Poetry and Prose,* ed. Donald H. Reiman and Neil Fraistat (New York: W. W. Norton, 2002), 498.

21. C. S. Lewis to Arthur Greeves, Sept. 12, 1933, in Lewis, *CL* II (San Francisco, Calif.: Harper, 2004), 121.

22. C. S. Lewis, *THS* (New York: Scribner, 2003), 176.

23. To attribute this sequence to the Space Trilogy does not imply that Lewis conceived it whole cloth in this manner from the outset. Based on the little evidence we have, it is more likely that the larger scheme emerged as the work progressed.

24. C. S. Lewis, "The Novels of Charles Williams," in his *OTOW,* ed. Walter Hooper (London: HarperCollins, 2000), 35.

25. Charles Williams, *Descent into Hell* (1937; Grand Rapids, Mich.: William B. Eerdmans Publishing Co., 1980), 16.

26. Lewis does not refer to the Gothic as such, but his own blend of the realistic and the supernatural is a virtual catalog of Gothic conventions: the pervasive atmosphere of "terror," "dread," and "horror" (the terms occur frequently); nightmares that record actual events otherwise unknown to the dreamer; imprisonment and persecution in the "haunted castle," the domain of oppressive authority; the interest in the relations between love and power, and the attendant problems of marriage, family, and inheritance in a changing but intractably patriarchal society; the creation of a "monster"—"that hideous strength"—associated with lust for the kind of knowledge that confers mastery over life itself; and the ancient crypt that marks the ever-present threat of a "return of the repressed"—the power of the past to haunt or invade the world of the living. The "beatific" transfiguration of the Gothic, derived from the fiction of Charles Williams, is evident in the "supernatural" shocks and surprises that constantly beset the modern sensibility of the heroine, Jane Studdock, and lead to her spiritual transformation; in the

manor of St. Anne's, which is not simply an avatar of medieval romance but a carefully crafted composite of traditional and modern elements that simultaneously sublimates and satirizes the "miserific" enchantment of Belbury; and in the redemptive action of Merlin the magician, who rises from the grave to exercise divine judgment (in a characteristically excessive Gothic manner) upon the dark powers that have sought to subdue to the planet. See Schwartz, *C. S. Lewis on the Final Frontier,* 91–140.

27. The difference between the beginning and the end of the Trilogy is especially instructive in this regard. In *Out of the Silent Planet,* Lewis responds to the evolutionary naturalism of H. G. Wells by constructing an imaginary world in which universal reason transcends the differences among the species and provides the basis for their mutual acknowledgment and shared participation in a divinely ordered cosmos. By contrast, in *That Hideous Strength,* where the enemy aspires to transcend the natural order itself, the transfiguration of the myth of "development" runs in the opposite direction. The emphasis is no longer on the rational harmony that transcends our animal nature but on the affirmation of our organic, embodied, and finite condition, or rather, the incarnate union of spirit and matter that constitutes our finite condition.

28. Lewis also describes this historical transformation as a process of "Internalisation" in which "century by century, item after item is transferred from the object's side of the account to the subject's." C. S. Lewis, *DI* (1964; Cambridge, UK: Cambridge Univ. Press, 1994), 215. Lewis's affection for the "discarded image" of premodern cosmology is apparent throughout his works, nowhere more so than in the volume of that title, where he declares "that the old Model delights me as I believe it delighted our ancestors. Few constructions of the imagination seem to me to have combined splendour, sobriety, and coherence in the same degree" (*DI,* 216). It is important to remember that Lewis follows this well-known statement first with the remark that, for all its appeal, this Medieval Model "had a serious defect; it was not true" (*DI,* 216); then with an examination of the interests, needs, and values behind the "new Model" that replaced it (*DI,* 219); and finally with a discussion of the manner and degree to which such relatively stable but impermanent "models" (roughly equivalent to the "paradigms" of Thomas Kuhn's groundbreaking study, *The Structure of Scientific Revolutions* [1963]) shape the particular forms of knowledge and the process of inquiry in each successive epoch.

29. Northrop Frye, *The Secular Scripture* (Cambridge, Mass.: Harvard Univ. Press, 1976), 142.

30. Richard Lancelyn Green and Walter Hooper, *C. S. Lewis: A Biography* (1974; revised and expanded ed., London: HarperCollins, 2002), 205.

Surprised by the Feminine

A Rereading of Gender Discourse in
C. S. Lewis's Perelandra

MONIKA B. HILDER

"Was C. S. Lewis sexist?" This question seems facile to many, and the common verdict is, "Indeed he was!" To some, he is a product of a sexist era, another "dead, white male poet" whose works should be approached with caution. After all, this is the man who in 1927 voted to limit the number of "wimmen" studying at Oxford.[1] His comments on "the masculine [as] the superior gender" are well known,[2] as are his fears that females will end the possibility of true male friendship.[3] His mock comments to E. R. Eddison, such as the one in a letter dated Nov. 16, 1942, on "som poore seely wench" who ought to make sport for her husband in his bed and bear children rather than pursue higher education (*CL* II, 535), are perhaps not so easily forgiven. The implications of an interchange during the coronation scene at the climax of *Perelandra* are likewise potentially troubling. When Queen Tinidril asks her husband first, "What are arches?" and then, "What are images?" and King Tor answers the first question, but bursts into laughter after the second question (*P*, 181), Kath Filmer, rather understandably, dismisses Tinidril as a "stupid" and "rather dense child" who requires male instruction.[4] But is *Perelandra* yet another example of C. S. Lewis's entrenched sexism? Of his apparent view that females tend to possess lesser cognitive ability?

    C. S. Lewis's fundamental celebration of medieval cosmology and, in particular, his imaginative investment in a hierarchical portrayal of gender, continues to spark debate. Undeniably, terms that in contemporary culture are subject to criticism and are most often disparaged in the spirit of postcolonialism—terms such as *patriarchy, hegemony, subordination, submission, domesticity, passivity,* and *obedience*—are the very metaphors that the old Oxford don applauded. Consequently, some scholars dismiss Lewis's imagination as anachronistic, concluding that his gender imagery is a reflection of his "theoretical dislike of the emancipated woman" and is an unfortunate, even dangerous form of indoctrination.[5] Fewer applaud what appears to some as his unequivocal position on women as beings of lesser capacity called to subordination.[6] More voices ponder the extent to which his apparent lapses into sexism may be separated from his affirmation of women and overall aesthetic and moral achievement.[7] But the argument that Lewis's medieval hierarchical metaphor for gender is *not* essentially sexist, but rather one that subverts and repairs sexism is usually overlooked.[8]

When Ransom first sees Tinidril, he realizes that "the green man was not a man at all, but a woman. It is difficult to say why this surprised him so. . . . But it did surprise him. . . . He had been expecting wonders, had been prepared for wonders, but not prepared for a goddess" (*P,* 47–48). The fact that otherworldly wonder should come in the feminine form challenges Ransom's ingrained paradigms. So perhaps we too might be surprised by Lewis's celebration of the "feminine." In this discussion, I will argue that Lewis's medieval imagination, or, more properly said, his own transformation of medieval imagination, challenges familiar Western paradigms of power and value in ways that may surprise and even liberate us from sexist oppression. Through a subversion of gender roles typically understood as oppressive, Lewis invites readers into considering gender metaphor in terms of spiritual and psychological empowerment for all humans.

As part of a continuing study on the body of Lewis's work, I will consider how *Perelandra* may be read in terms of the root metaphors of the two competing heroic models of Western thinking: classical heroism, embodying the traditionally viewed "masculine" values of reason, autonomy, activity, aggression, and pride, and the lesser understood, often subjugated, spiritual heroism, embodying the traditionally viewed "feminine" values of imagination, interdependence, passivity, care, and humility. This is informed by my reading of Milton's depiction of heroic models in *Paradise Lost.* Although Lewis is frequently assessed as guilty of sexism, he may, in fact, be regarded as an advocate of "theological feminism" who subverts the classical model of heroism with his celebration of the so-called "feminine" nature of spiritual power.[9] In particular, I will explore the problem of classical "masculine" classical heroism posed in Weston, the Un-man, and the solution offered by the "feminine" spiritual heroism developing in Ransom. Questions surrounding the issue of jihad, as well as the characterizations of Tinidril, Tor, Mars, and Venus, and the cosmic dance will also be considered.

WESTON, THE UN-MAN: "MASCULINE" CLASSICAL HEROISM

The physicist, Dr. Weston, embodies the traditionally viewed "masculine" values of classical heroism: autonomy, aggression, and pride. As his name suggests, Weston represents the height of Western humanism, or rather its demise in the amoral "new man," the Nietzschean superman.

In an allusion to Lucifer, Weston arrives on Perelandra "like a shooting star" falling from Deep Heaven (*P,* 65–66). Ransom, we learn, "could hardly help admiring [Weston's] massive egoism which enabled [him] in the very moment of his arrival on an unknown world to stand there unmoved in all his authoritative vulgarity, his arms akimbo, his face scowling, and his feet planted as solidly on that unearthly soil as if he had been . . . in his own study" (*P,* 74). His sole purpose on Perelandra is to seduce Tinidril to exchange living on the Floating Islands in "feminine" dependence on Maleldil for living on the Fixed Land in "masculine" self-reliance.[10] In language typical of Western chauvinism's commitment to classical heroism, Weston challenges her to adopt the supremacy of self-will. Tinidril is to leave her current "smallness" in order to become "very great . . . very wise . . . very courageous" (*P,* 102–3). Mocking a life of so-called "mere childbearing" (*P,* 112), Weston instead projects the "phantom self"(*P,* 118) of personal greatness.

In a sense it is almost hard to think of Weston as a classical hero. With near lightning speed he deteriorates into something vulgar, really more of an embarrassment to classical heroism than an affirmation of its glory. He makes crude jokes and displays sheer and wanton cruelty to frogs. What has this figure, with "a whole repertory of obscenities to perform" (*P,* 110), to do with classical grandeur? But Weston's deterioration should be regarded as the logical outcome of classical heroism. Just as the fallen angels in *Paradise Lost* show early signs of degeneration, Weston's impressive stance is short-lived. Self-reliance cannot be sustained. After a lifelong stance of classical "masculine" autonomy, Weston embraces the ultimately ironic "feminine" role of surrender to the Life-Force (or rather, the Death-Force): as he says, he is "being made a fit receptacle" for this power (*P,* 81) and calls this "Force" into himself (*P,* 82).

The diabolical possession of what was once Weston is now complete, and for the greater part of the story the annihilated Weston, as the term *Un-man* signifies, illustrates the impossibility of ultimate autonomy in a moral universe. In such a universe, the "masculine" grasp for power implodes upon itself.

RANSOM: "FEMININE" SPIRITUAL HEROISM

In Elwin Ransom, Lewis explores the solution to the temptation of classical heroism. As his name implies—Elwin, "the friend of the eldila" (*P,* 167), and Ransom, the Savior by substitution after the nature of Maleldil himself—he embodies the traditionally viewed "feminine" values of spiritual heroism: interdependence, passivity, and humility. But this spiritual heroism is an emerging process; at first Ransom appears as an unlikely hero of either paradigm.

Unlike larger-than-life classical heroes, Ransom has little that is remarkable about him. He was, the reader learns, "a timid creature, a man who shrank back from new and hard things" (*P,* 104). While Professor Weston arrives as a resolute conqueror, Professor Ransom is "a tall, white, shivering, weary scarecrow of a man" (*P,* 26) who is whisked away to the unknown like a parcel. He inspires peals of laughter in the Green Lady. He experiences "shame" because "he kn[ows] his body to be a little ugly and a little ridiculous" (*P,* 52). He discerns that he, like "ordinary people" everywhere, is fighting in a cosmic battle against dark powers and principalities (*P,* 21), and a "terrible sense of inadequacy" (*P,* 70) overwhelms him. He complains of the unfairness that he, "a man of straw" (*P,* 121), should be in this "preposterous" (*P,* 121) position of "fight[ing] the immortal enemy" when he, "a sedentary scholar," has never won a fight in his life (*P,* 124). The unlikelihood of his success, as seen from a classical paradigm, is clear in the Un-man's subsequent taunt: "you think, little one, that you can fight with me?"(*P,* 130). Ransom will either utterly fail, or else supersede classical heroism in unforeseen ways.

One might ask, what makes this cowardly man courageous? The "hideous" (*P,* 26) "coffin-like chariot" (*P,* 166) provided for his travel is a clue: Ransom undergoes the death to his ego. This "feminine" submission to the "masculine" divine is the key. Though terrified of the seemingly impossible task of overcoming the diabolical enemy, Ransom grasps hold of the utterly surprising idea that he is the miraculous "representative" of Maleldil (*P,* 120–21). He looks beyond the dubious position of "his ridiculous piebald body and . . . ten times defeated arguments" (*P,* 120), and accepts the enormity of his moral role in the cosmic pattern. Ransom is an echo of the divine, who submitted Himself to the incarnation, with its final humiliation in the crucifixion; similarly, Ransom regards his body as an "instrument" which he "surrender[s]" to the battle (*P,* 128). In contrast to Weston, whose identity is "melted" into the satanic demise (*P,* 148), Ransom looks forward to the consummation in which he will find his true self: as he says to himself of God, "'When I wake up after Thy image, I shall be satisfied'" (*P,* 128). Ransom's ethos of "feminine" surrender, paradoxically, is what empowers him with unparalleled courage against the foe.

This of course quickly brings us to the troublesome issue of jihad. For one thing, waging a holy war against a spiritual enemy is fraught with features that we easily identify with classical heroism—active combat, conquest, even personal glory for the victor. Can the murder of the Un-man possibly be understood as moral and illustrative of spiritual heroism? Perhaps the raw physical violence brings to mind Philip Pullman's claim that the *Chronicles of Narnia* illustrate Lewis's congenital preference for violence? But before we regard this jihad as a lapse into typical classical heroism, we should note Ransom's own distaste for physical battle: "It stood to reason," he thinks, "that a struggle with the Devil meant a *spiritual* struggle . . . the notion of a physical combat was only fit for a savage. . . . no such crude, materialistic struggle could possibly be what Maleldil really intended" (*P,* 122). However, Ransom realizes that the "unhappy division between soul and body" is an erroneous result of the Fall (*P,* 122), and that in his soul/body he has been called as an agent of Maleldil to end the temptation of Tinidril. His battle is no longer against Weston but against the diabolical Un-man—what is no longer human but only "an instrument. . . .

at the disposal of a furious self-exiled negation" (*P,* 132). As Lewis writes elsewhere, "We are not asked to love the damned. When the fiend's victim has wholly ceased to be human, when his will is no longer merely dominated by but unrecoverably identified with, his rider, charity is no longer commanded. But we are not allowed to assume that this has taken place in any man still alive, and obviously we don't know enough."[11] Ransom's physical battle with the Un-man may be understood as a transformation of the classical heroic paradigm.[12] Whereas the wrath of Achilles and the martial valor of all classical heroes is ego-driven and bound to obtaining secular glories, Ransom discovers "the joy [that] came from finding at last what hatred was made for" when directed against the ancient foe (*P,* 132).

The physical battle waged between Ransom and the Un-man is thus an image of the "war in heaven" described in Revelation 12. Ransom's jihad is best regarded as a symbolic manifestation of what is acted out in the spiritual realm; it is not to be confused with the practice of jihad on the sociopolitical level and, indeed, Lewis warns against equating purely spiritual evil with an individual or a political cause.[13] Ransom recognizes how easily this distinction is misunderstood, describing this as "an experience that perhaps no good man can ever have in our world . . . a torrent of perfectly unmixed and lawful hatred" (*P,* 132). Moreover, the murder of Un-man using Weston's body is even depicted as an act of mercy that honors the former Weston[14]—the very antithesis of the spirit of jihad that solely identifies the human with the demonic.

Ransom's essential "feminine" heroism centered in the divine is underscored in everything that follows his battle with Un-man. Unlike the classical hero, who glories in the victory of his own strength, Ransom is in a state of extreme weakness and dependence. Like a child being born, he is expelled from the cave as from a womb. "He lay helpless, in the end, rushing forward through echoing darkness," and then "was rushed out into broad daylight and air and warmth, and rolled head over heels, and deposited, dazzled and breathless, in the shallows of a great pool"(*P,* 158). There he undergoes "convalescence. . . . a second infancy, in which he was breast-fed by the planet Venus herself" (*P,* 159). Similarly, when Ransom learns on coronation day that all is well, he faints (*P,* 169). Malacandra responds with the paradoxical praise that is at once a disclaimer befitting the spiritual hero: "'Be comforted. It is no doing of yours. You are not great, though you could have prevented a thing so great that Deep Heaven sees it with amazement. Be comforted, small one, in your smallness. He lays no merit on you. Receive and be glad. Have no fear, lest your shoulders be bearing this world. Look! it is beneath your head and carries you'" (*P,* 169) And although Ransom is also honored with such titles as "Lord and Father" (*P,* 178), "Friend and Saviour" (*P,* 190), and Maleldil's chief instrument (*P,* 178), this praise does not merit pride. As Ransom articulates prior to the journey, spiritual heroism precludes hubris: "One never can see, or not till long afterwards, why *any* one was selected for *any* job. And when one does, it is usually some reason that leaves no room for vanity" (*P,* 22). The wound in his heel inflicted by the Un-man signifies Ransom's Christlike act of substitution; the fact that this wound continues to bleed shows the intrinsic weakness by which spiritual victory is won.

Elwin Ransom embodies the paradoxical power and victory of spiritual heroism. Out of the "feminine" ethos of submission to the divine, Ransom enacts conquest of the demonic. His story illustrates that in a moral universe the "feminine" abdication of personal power results in dynamic victory over evil.

PERELANDRAN CHARACTERS, TINIDRIL AND TOR, VENUS AND MARS; THE COSMIC DANCE

The emerging and decisive victory of Ransom's spiritual heroism over Weston's familiar classical heroism is the main action of the novel, at least as important as, if not more important than, its main subject—the temptation of Tinidril and possible fall of this planet. And it is only in the light of Lewis's subversion of the classical paradigm of personal power and conquest that the novel's informing metaphor, the cosmic dance, can be understood. I turn my attention now to how Lewis's characterization of the human pair, the angelic beings, and the central image of the cosmic dance itself challenges the ways in which we perceive power, identity, and value.

THE HUMAN PAIR, TINIDRIL AND TOR

While it is typical in gender discourse to speak of husband and wife as separate beings engaged in a power struggle, one in which males have historically exercised egotistical dominance over females, Lewis has instead tried to depict an unfallen world in which husband and wife illustrate mystical union. So while we are understandably disposed to thinking of females as the dominated ones who have been acculturated into weaker or silent roles—politically, intellectually, and emotionally—and therefore easily read Tinidril's questions to Tor, "What are arches?" and "What are images?" (*P,* 181), as evidence that Lewis regarded females as intellectually inferior,[15] Lewis challenges this sexism. We expect Lewis to depict the queen as the king's intellectual inferior, but in fact the king has gained his rational knowledge through her. Quite playfully, Lewis transcends the familiar notion of gendered intellectual power relations, in which so-called "masculine reason" engenders knowledge. In this case, Tinidril has the typically "masculine" role of begetting knowledge and Tor the "feminine" role of bearing knowledge. As with Milton's angels, Tinidril's intuition engenders rational human knowledge, and it is clear, as Tor claims, that "All is gift" (*P,* 180).[16] No independent human strength gives value to persons or plays the decisive role in winning the battle against sin. Egotistical pride fails. Humanistic reason is dethroned. True power and identity are seen in relationship—the interdependence of the human couple and their obedience to Maleldil.

Together Tor and Tinidril represent "the very daughter [voice] of *the Voice*" (*P,* 177; emphasis added), the feminine response of obedience to the divine voice. Together they also represent the masculine authority over the planet. Perelandra's greeting emphasizes their plurality-in-unity: "Hail . . . oh man and woman, Oyarsa-Perelendri, *the Adam, the Crown,* Tor and Tinidril" (*P,* 177; emphasis added). Ransom recognizes this mystery: "Paradise itself in its two Persons, Paradise walking hand in hand" (*P,* 175). The at once hilarious but also deeply solemn image of the united couple lifting "its male right hand" underscores Lewis's sense that their royal power is a complementary whole, perfect, life-giving, not marred by the patterns of dominance and enslavement we typically associate with power and divisive gender relations. Ransom recognizes them as "the resolution of discords, the bridge that spans what would else be a chasm in creation, the keystone of the whole arch" (*P,* 178). By contrast, fallen men and women appear to Ransom as "shadows and broken images" (*P,* 176). Whereas the classical heroic emphasizes the gender divide in terms of competitive egos in warfare, the spiritual heroic applauds the harmonious interdependence of individuals glorifying their Maker. It is the meek, not the proud, who inherit the planet.

THE ANGELIC BEINGS, VENUS AND MARS

Similarly, Lewis's depiction of Venus and Mars illustrates the ethos of humility. Individually, each represents cosmic Femininity and Masculinity. However, Lewis resists reducing gender to biology,[17] and we experience these gender archetypes as "'trans-sexual'" (*P,* 30). Moreover, gender neither limits nor enhances the integrity of their being or their effective leadership over their respective planets. The key is that together their characters affirm the *feminine* relation to the divine. Both are servants of Maleldil; both practice the paradox of empowering humility. Both are servant-leaders whose authority is founded on obedience. It is "their glory and their joy" to cherish and teach Tinidril and Tor until they in turn become greater (*P,* 71).[18] At the coronation scene these huge eldila gladly bow before "the small forms of [the] young King and Queen" (*P,* 175). As Lewis writes in *The Four Loves,* "they 'are taller when they bow.'"[19]

THE COSMIC DANCE

Finally, the cosmic dance, the informing metaphor of the novel, illustrates Lewis's subversion of classical heroism. Here he celebrates a medieval-inspired vision of hierarchical order in which every aspect of creation has its destined place in the grand design. In feudalism, as in its metaphor of the "chain of being," roles are defined, identity is prescribed, and obedience is a key virtue. Beyond Earth's moon, this grand cosmic dance is unbroken: all participate in one harmonious paean of praise. But whereas feudalism and the "chain of being" is associated with rigid hierarchy and abusive power relations, Lewis's ideal or transformed vision of hierarchy is defined by a fluidity in which every other aspect of creation is at the center because Maleldil is the center.[20] This is the biblical paradox that challenges ordinary Western logic: to abdicate is to receive power, to bow is to rise, to mirror the other is indeed to find one's self.[21]

Therefore the growing list of "bad" words that we often associate with abusive power relations—words such as *patriarchy, hegemony, subordination, submission, domesticity, passivity,* and *obedience*—need to be rethought in Lewis's works. Arguably, his intention is to redeem these metaphors, take them from their original classical context (e.g., *hegemony* originally was used in reference to political predominance of one group over another in ancient Greece), and situate them rightly in the cosmic dance. Startlingly to modern ears, it is through "hegemony" and "subordination" that all parts of the universe participate in a festivity of Joy. Ransom experiences the "intertwining undulation" of the Great Dance in terms of a hegemony in which each figure becomes the focal point in his vision only to be entangled again by another figure. But in this hegemony, "the former pattern [was] not thereby dispossessed but finding in its new subordination a significance greater than that which it had abdicated" (*P,* 187). Dominion occurs without oppression; submission enables dominion; dominion abdicates and regains self. We learn, "All is righteousness and there is no equality. . . . as when stones support and are supported in an arch, such is His order; rule and obedience, begetting and bearing" (*P,* 184).

In this Great Dance or Game, "Each grain is at the centre. The Dust is at the centre. The Worlds are at the centre. . . . Each thing, from the single grain of Dust to the strongest eldil, is the end and the final cause of all creation and the mirror in which the beam of His brightness comes to rest and so returns to Him. Blessed be He!" (*P,* 185–6). Similarly, in *Mere Christianity* Lewis speaks of God as "not . . . static . . . but [as] a dynamic, pulsating activity, a life, almost a kind of drama. . . . The whole dance, or drama, or pattern of this three-Personal life is to be played out in each one of us: or (putting it the other way round) each one of us has got to enter that pattern, take his place in that dance. There is no other way to the happiness for which we were made."[22] Tinidril and Tor are such dancers, as are Mars and Venus (*P,* 175). Ransom, notably, very confused by this fluid hierarchy, finds he does not know the identities of the many speakers, although he thinks that he himself is also one of them (*P,* 183). Humor abounds! This cosmic dance, which "does not wait to be perfect" (*P,* 183) and in which all things kneel and bow and rise and, in a sense, reign, replaces destructive conceptions of power with a life-giving one.

In conclusion, Lewis, in his transformation of medieval hierarchy, poses possibilities for gender discourse that deserve further investigation. As he concluded in *The Discarded Image,* "I hope no one will think that I am recommending a return to the Medieval Model. I am only suggesting considerations that may induce us to regard all Models in the right way, respecting each and idolising none."[23] His treatment of gender metaphor in *Perelandra* perhaps poses a remarkable achievement in ironic subversion and restoration that has wide-reaching implications. It is likely that

Lewis himself would have been surprised. His holistic vision suggests a theological feminism of humility toward the divine and, therefore, between humans, that postcolonial discourse has yet to consider. For Lewis, the cosmos is a dance of infinite interlocking patterns that are all "linked and looped together by the unions of a kneeling with a sceptred love. Blessed be He!" (*P*, 186).

Notes

1. C. S. Lewis to W. H. Lewis, July 9, 1927, in Lewis, *CL* I (New York: Harper-SanFrancisco, 2000), 703.

2. C. S. Lewis, *PPL* (London: Oxford Univ. Press, 1974), 113.

3. C. S. Lewis to Dom Bede Griffiths, May 26, 1943, in Lewis, *CL* II (New York: HarperSanFrancisco, 2004), 577. In this same letter, Lewis says (in reference to Dom Bede's comments on landscape and comparison to Dante), "Perhaps you also took Perelandra too seriously. Although the theme has serious implications, it is primarily a 'yarn'" (576).

4. C. S. Lewis, *P* (New York: Scribner, 2003); Kath Filmer, *The Fiction of C. S. Lewis: Mask and Mirror* (London: Macmillan, 1993), 99.

5. Gretchen Bartels, "Of Men and Mice: C. S. Lewis on Male-Female Interactions," *Literature and Theology* 22, no. 3 (Sept. 2008): 324–38 (quotation, 324); and see Filmer, *Fiction of C. S. Lewis*; Candice Fredrick and Sam McBride, *Women Among the Inklings: Gender, C. S. Lewis, J. R. R. Tolkien, and Charles Williams* (Westport, Conn.: Greenwood Press, 2001); and Mary Stewart Van Leeuwen, *A Sword Between the Sexes? C. S. Lewis and the Gender Debates* (Grand Rapids, Mich.: Brazos Press, 2010), passim.

6. See Adam Barkman, "'All is Righteousness and there is no Equality': C. S. Lewis on Gender and Justice," *Christian Scholar's Review* 36, no. 4 (Summer 2007): 415–36.

7. See, for example, Corbin Scott Carnell, "The Meaning of Masculine and Feminine in the Work of C. S. Lewis," *Modern British Literature* 2 (1977): 153–59; David C. Downing, *Planets in Peril: A Critical Study of C. S. Lewis's Ransom Trilogy* (Amherst, Mass.: Univ. of Massachusetts Press, 1992); Paul F. Ford, *Companion to Narnia* (1980; New York: HarperSanFrancisco, 1994); Doris T. Meyers, "Brave New World: The Status of Women According to Tolkien, Lewis, and Williams," *Cimarron Review* 17 (Oct. 1971): 13–19; Doris T. Myers, "Lewis in Genderland," *Christian Scholar's Review* 36, no. 4 (Summer 2007): 455–60; and Jennifer Swift, "'A More Fundamental Reality than Sex': C. S. Lewis and the Hierarchy of Gender," *The Chronicle of the Oxford University C. S. Lewis Society* 5, no. 1 (2008): 5–26.

8. Although Jennifer Swift does regard Lewis as a kind of chauvinist, she argues that he transformed the conventional understanding of male headship in a modern way (Swift, "'A More Fundamental Reality than Sex,'" 21).

9. I have explored this in "The Foolish Weakness in C. S. Lewis's Cosmic Trilogy: A Feminine Heroic," *Seven: An Anglo-American Literary Review* 19 (2002): 77–90; in *Educating the Moral Imagination: The Fantasy Literature of George MacDonald, C. S. Lewis, and Madeleine L'Engle* (Ph.D. thesis, Simon Fraser University, 2003; in *The Feminine Ethos in C. S. Lewis's* Chronicles of Narnia (New York: Peter Lang, 2012); in *The Gender Dance: Ironic Subversion in C. S. Lewis's Cosmic Trilogy* (New York, 2013); and in *Surprised by the Feminine: A Rereading of C. S. Lewis and Gender* (New York, Peter Lang, in press).

10. The Floating Islands are a metaphor of ultimate trust in Maleldil, signifying living in the moment, in gratitude, in humility. Maleldil had forbidden Tor and Tinidril to live on the Fixed Land (*P,* 89), and Weston/ Un-Man rightly perceives that the choice to disobey would signify Tinidril's independence of Tor, and ultimately of Maleldil, in a classical grasp for egotistical, self-determined power. Tor speaks of rejecting the wave as "cold love and feeble trust" (*P,* 179). After the temptation has been withstood and removed, however, another Fixed Land with its holy mountain, Tai Harendrimar, The Hill of Life (181), designed by Perelandra under Maleldil's instruction (*P,* 168), will be the home of Tor and Tinidril's royal throne (*P,* 181). Ransom recognizes that "*this* island had never been forbidden them, and that one purpose in forbidding the other had been to lead them to this their destined throne" (*P,* 174). The Un-Man speaks partial truth in his temptation that living on the Fixed Land will signify Tinidril's wisdom and freedom to choose. He does not understand that the path to the Fixed Land is the ethos of abdication and humility, and that this is the Perelandran pair's destiny.

11. C. S. Lewis to W. H. Lewis, May 4, 1940, in Lewis, *CL* II, 409.

12. Although my main argument is that Lewis shares Milton's vision of Satan as the epitome of classical heroism in which the ego-bound individual ultimately fails, it is also true that Lewis regarded the pagan myths in terms of inklings of the divine, messages sent by the Landlord, God, to prepare humanity throughout history for the fulfillment of revelation in the incarnation. Thus, while classical heroism at core is at odds with spiritual heroism, its celebration of values such as activity and even hatred points to true heroism. Similarly, Christ in Milton's depiction of the war in heaven has been described as an "Achilles-like hero." Barbara Kiefer Lewalski, "The Genres of *Paradise Lost*," in *The Cambridge Companion to Milton*, ed. Dennis Danielson (Cambridge, UK: Cambridge Univ. Press, 2008), 125.

13. Lewis was no pacifist and believed in fighting against Germany in both world wars. He speaks of fighting Hitler as the right cause. But—to argue against Pullman's view of Lewis's apparent congenital preference for violence—in discussing the Battle of Britain Lewis makes an important distinction between spiritual wickedness and humanity's various sociopolitical affiliations. In 1940 he warned against "identifying the [German and Russian] enemy with the forces of evil," spoke

of praying for Hitler and Stalin, and pondered that "one of the things we learn from history is that God never allows a human conflict to become unambiguously one between simple good and simple evil?" (C. S. Lewis to Dom Bede Griffiths, Apr. 16, 1940, in Lewis, *CL* II, 391). Similarly, in his declaration that "charity is no longer commanded" for the damned, he warns, "we are not allowed to assume that this has taken place in any man still alive" (C. S. Lewis to W. H. Lewis, May 4, 1940, in Lewis, *CL* II, 409).

14. The reader learns that "the idea that something which had once been of his own kind and fed at a human breast might even now be imprisoned in the thing he was pursuing redoubled his hatred, which . . . increased his strength" (*P,* 133). Similarly, Ransom's subsequent grave marker to Weston is a tribute to his former humanity (*P,* 161)—in contradistinction to the spirit of jihad.

15. See, for example, Filmer, *The Fiction of C. S. Lewis,* 99.

16. In Milton's *Paradise Lost,* in reference to Adam's typical use of reason in contrast with Eve's typical use of intuition, Raphael cites angelic reason as intuitive, and his musing about intuitive angelic reason as the possible reward for obedience challenges typical perceptions of gender hierarchy (John Milton, *Paradise Lost* (1674), in *John Milton: Complete Poems and Major Prose,* ed. Merritt Y. Hughes [Indianapolis, Ind.: Odyssey, 1976], book 5: 485–503). Similarly, in his poem *The Prelude,* Wordsworth hails "Imagination" as "Reason . . . exalted" (William Wordsworth, The Prelude [1850], in *Selected Poems and Prefaces,* ed. Jack Stillinger [Boston: Houghton Mifflin, 1965], book 14, lines 189–92). Questions as to which sort of knowledge is superior or which gender is doing what sort of thinking are irrelevant in the mystery of interdependent harmony. To ask the question is like a blunder that interrupts the dance.

17. This modernist reduction is symptomatic of philosophical materialism. In Peter Kreeft's words, "how can sex be sacred unless it is cosmic?" (Peter Kreeft, "The Joyful Cosmology: *Perelandra's* 'Great Dance' as an Alternative World View to Modern Reductionism," in his *C. S. Lewis for the Third Millenium* [San Francisco, Calif: Ignatius, 1994], 173). In the characters Mars and Venus, Lewis creates a paradoxical affirmation of gender that is also a subversion. Ransom notes the inadequacy of language to convey such a mystery: "It is words that are vague. The reason why the thing can't be expressed is that it's too *definite* for language" (*P,* 30). Their bodies are "free from any sexual characteristics, either primary or secondary" (*P,* 171). But although "'trans-sexual'" (*P,* 30), the planetary spirits are also examples of gender essentialism. "The Oyarsa of Mars," readers learn, "shone with cold and morning colours, a little metallic—pure, hard, and bracing. The Oyarsa of Venus glowed with a warm splendour, full of the suggestion of teeming vegetable life" (*P,* 171). As the narrator explains, "Gender is a reality, and a more fundamental reality than sex. Sex is, in fact, merely the adaptation to organic life of a fundamental polarity which divides all created beings" (*P,* 172). Thus, while Lewis affirms the ancient polarization of gender, he also, quite radically, subverts the typical dichotomization of sexuality in which difference is understood in terms

of sexist subjugation of the female. The apparent "sword between the sexes," to be reconciled through marriage in which "the two become fully human," as we see in Tor and Tinidril, is better understood as a paradoxical "carnival of sexuality [which] *leads us out beyond our sexes*"(C. S. Lewis, *AGO* [New York: Bantam, 1976], 57–58; emphasis added).

18. Moreover, on unfallen Perelandra, their power is lesser because the human pair has direct access to Maleldil.

19. C. S. Lewis, *FL* (London: Fontana, 1974), 109; Lewis acknowledges G. K. Chesterton in the idea that they are "'taller when they bow.'"

20. In Peter Kreeft's words, "What, then, is the center? . . . The answer is: everything and nothing. Everything, because of the divine immanence; nothing, because of the divine transcendence" (Kreeft, "Joyful Cosmology," 184).

21. The hilarity of the cosmic dance is already anticipated in the carnival atmosphere of the animals arriving for the royal celebration: mostly in pairs, male and female, the beasts and birds are seen "fawning upon one another, climbing over one another, diving under one another's bellies, [and] perching upon one another's backs" (*P,* 174). Gender is essential; hierarchy is the cosmic order; but these differences-in-unity suggest wonder, liberty, and life.

22. C. S. Lewis, *MC* (London: Fontana, 1974), 148–49.

23. C. S. Lewis, *DI* (Cambridge: Cambridge Univ. Press, 1964), 222.

The Center and the Rim

Inversions of the System of the Heavens in Perelandra *and* The Discarded Image

NIKOLAY EPPLÉE

The writings of C. S. Lewis are deeply interrelated. Of special interest for the cultural historian are the relations between his scholarly and fictional works. They closely comment on one another: *The Allegory of Love* (written in parallel with the allegory *Pilgrim's Regress*) is, in a way, a collection of images later expressed in the symbolism of Narnia. *A Preface to Paradise Lost* is likewise closely interconnected with the complex of moral problems treated in *Mere Christianity* (then being delivered as a series of radio talks), and provides an important parallel to the theme of Adam and Eve in *Perelandra*. *The Discarded Image* is a late Lewisian manifesto on the advantage of the medieval model over modernity, and in a way a historical subtext to his antimodernism.[1] But the parallels between Lewis's Cosmic or Space Trilogy and his "philological trilogy" constitute an especially fructuous and beautiful theme.

Here is just one example (though a very important one) of interrelations between *Perelandra* and *The Discarded Image*. In the final chapter of *Perelandra*, the hero, a modest philologist who has become a ransomer of the Venusian version of sacred history, contemplates and joins the Great Dance, a visionary résumé of the novel. One of its leitmotifs is the theme of center and periphery, the center and the rim. Ransom first introduces this motif when he confesses that the recent events on Perelandra confound his cherished belief in the centrality of the human race, and thus bring uncomfortably close

the enemy's talk which thrusts my world and my race into a remote corner
and gives me a universe with no center at all, but millions of worlds that
lead nowhere or (what is worse) to more and more worlds for ever, and
comes over me with numbers and empty spaces and repetitions and asks
me to bow down before bigness. . . . Is the enemy easily answered when
He says that all is without plan or meaning? As soon as we think we see
one it melts away into nothing, or into some other plan that we never
dreamed of, and what was the center becomes the rim, till we doubt if
any shape or plan or pattern was ever more than a trick of our own eyes,
cheated with hope, or tired with too much looking.[2]

But peering into the Dance, Ransom perceives that

Each grain is at the center. The Dust is at the center. The Worlds are at
the center. The beasts are at the center. The ancient peoples are there. The
race that sinned is there. . . . Where Maleldil is, there is the center. He is in
every place. Not some of Him in one place and some in another, but in each
place the whole Maleldil, even in the smallness beyond thought. There is
no way out of the center save into the Bent Will which casts itself into the
Nowhere. . . . Each thing was made for Him. He is the center. Because we
are with Him, each of us is at the center. . . . There seems no plan because
it is all plan: there seems no center because it is all center. (*P,* 216–18)

Earlier in the novel, in the fascinating scene of Ransom's visible battle
with the Un-Man, Lewis introduces a seductive, "bent" image of the universe. Another earthman, seduced and turned into Satan's emissary and
embodiment, introduces Ransom to his master's worldview: "All the good
things are now—a thin little rind of what we call life, put on for show,
and then—the real universe for ever and ever. . . . *all* the dead have sunk
down into the inner darkness: under the rind. . . . Picture the universe
as an infinite globe with this very thin crust on the outside" (*P,* 167–68).
And God is outside this Globe, "like a Moon." He is transcendent in the
sense that He does not care for and never follows his creatures sinking
into nonentity.

This model of the universe is not merely the Un-Man's drivel. It is a
medieval universe from the corrupt creature's point of view. Comparing

the quoted description of the Great Dance with the Un-Man's globe, we can see that the unfallen world of Perelandra, open to Deep Heaven, contrasts with its inverted, "bent" image, a thin rind that is dark inside.

It is instructive to analyze this inversion, as well as the parallels between the Perelandran universe and the medieval one, in the light of the startlingly revealing cosmological construction of Lewis's monograph *The Discarded Image*, which may be regarded as his scholarly testament. Here, the system of the heavens is described as part of the medieval model, the world-image (*Weltanschauung*) of medieval man. From Plato's *Timaeus* onward, the movement of the Heavens was the paradigm for the movements of the soul and "moral law inwards." Lewis acknowledges that he is enchanted by the model and, above all, by its most complete and ingenious embodiment in Dante's *Divina Commedia*. For Lewis, as a historian of literature, the historical transmutation of *Himmelsanschauung* from the medieval model to the modern one amounts to a changeover from a Dantean to a Miltonian tradition.[3] The medieval vision of the world is holistic and hierarchic. Unlike the Newtonian universe of modernity, the medieval universe has an absolute up and down, center and periphery: physical space correlates here with moral dimension.

> Whatever else a modern feels when he looks at the night sky, he certainly feels that he is looking *out*—like one looking out from the saloon entrance on to the dark Atlantic or from the lighted porch upon dark and lonely moors. But if you accepted the Medieval Model you would feel like one looking *in*. The Earth is "outside the city wall". When the Sun is up he dazzles us and we cannot see inside. Darkness, our own darkness, draws the veil and we catch a glimpse of the high pomps within; the vast, lighted concavity filled with music and life.... Then, laying aside whatever Theology or Atheology you held before, run your mind up heaven by heaven to Him who is really the center, to your senses the circumference, of all. (*DI*, 18–19)[4]

Lewis, as it were, inverts the modern scheme: dark and inhuman space, without a center, turns out to be the glorious Heavens whose center is God. This closely echoes the Dantean inversion in *Paradiso* 28. Rising to the Ninth Heaven, Beatrice and Dante contemplate the prototype of the material universe, the Divine Point with pyreal circles revolving around:

About this Point a fiery circle whirled,
With such rapidity it had outraced
The swiftest spheres revolving round the world.

This by another circle was embraced,
This by a third, which yet a fourth enclosed;
Round this a fifth, round that a sixth I traced.

Beyond, the seventh was so wide disclosed
That Iris, to enfold it were too small,
Her rainbow a full circle being supposed.

So too the eighth and ninth; and each and all
More slowly turned as they were more removed
Numerically from the integral.

Purest in flame the inmost circle proved.
Being nearest the Pure Spark, or so I venture,
Most clearly with Its truth it is engrooved.[5]

Precisely as a contemplative model, an intellectual construct, the model of the medieval Heavens can be inverted (the term being quite convenient as we can also speak here about a chord inversion in the harmony of spheres). The Empyrean, the spatial periphery, the "rim," which is in fact the moral and intellectual center, in the *Commedia* also turns out to be a visual center. To Dante's question "why copy from its pattern goes awry," Beatrice answers that the largesse of a sphere in the visual—material—heaven corresponds in the intellectual world to the force (*virtù*) of the fiery ring, which is greater the closer it is to the energy and spiritual Center, the Divine Point.[6]

Describing this inversion, Lewis here repeatedly acts as an illusionist: he tries not just to explain the case but to boggle the reader's imagination.

Nothing is more deeply impressed on the cosmic imaginings of a modern than the idea that the heavenly bodies move in a pitch-black and dead-cold vacuity. It was not so in the Medieval Model. . . . the ascending spirit passes into a region compared with which our terrestrial day is only a sort of night; and nowhere in medieval literature have I found any suggestion that, if we could enter the translunary world, we should find ourselves in an abyss of darkness. For their system is in one sense more heliocentric than ours. The sun illuminates the whole universe. . . . Night is merely the conical shadow cast by our Earth. . . . When we look up at the night sky we are looking through darkness but not at darkness. (*DI*, 111–12)

No wonder that the theme, so vivid for Lewis as a scholar, is of so much importance for him in his theology and fiction. Platonic-Augustinian admiration for the divine nature and unfallen creation as *realissima* compared to sensible reality is the landmark of his theology and, in fact, of all of his thought. The effect of joyful disappointment—*eucatastrophe*, to use Tolkien's term—the very same as we experienced looking beyond the Moon's orbit, is his fundamental emotion.[7] This very emotion colors the entire trilogy. Everyone who has ever read the first book of the Cosmic Trilogy remembers Ransom's excitement when he first contemplates Heaven, having come out of the silent planet:

But Ransom, as time wore on, became aware of another and more spiritual cause for his progressive lightening and exultation of heart. A nightmare, long engendered in the modern mind by the mythology that follows in the wake of science, was falling off him. He had read of "Space": at the back of his thinking for years had lurked the dismal fancy of the black, cold vacuity, the utter deadness, which was supposed to separate the worlds. He had not known how much it affected him till now—now that the very name "Space" seemed a blasphemous libel for this empyrean ocean of radiance in which they swam. He could not call it "dead"; he felt life pouring into him from it every moment. How indeed should it be otherwise, since out of this ocean the worlds and all their life had come? He had thought it barren; he saw now that it was the womb of all worlds, whose blazing and innumerable offspring looked down nightly even upon the earth with so many eyes—and here, with how many more! No: space was the wrong name. Older thinkers had been wiser when they named it simply the heavens—the heavens which declare the glory—the
happy climes that lie
Where day never shuts his eye,
Up in the broad fields of the sky.[8]

Several pages later we find this theme and this mechanism of inversion further elaborated:

> [Ransom] wondered how he could ever have thought of planets, even of the Earth, as islands of life and reality floating in a deadly void. Now, with a certainty which never after deserted him, he saw the planets . . . as mere holes or gaps in the living heaven . . . And yet, he thought, beyond the solar system the brightness ends. Is that the real void, the real death? Unless . . . he groped for the idea . . . unless visible light is also a hole or gap, a mere diminution of something else. Something that is to bright unchanging heaven as heaven is to the dark, heavy earths. (*OSP*, 53)

It is the very mechanism of the Dantean in. . ⌣. ⌣ion in *Paradiso* 28: from a physical centrifugal model to a metaphysical and centripetal one. The center and the rim motif leads us here to yet another metamorphosis of the model of the universe, also quite familiar to Lewis. The Dantean universe, with its stable and spiritual center, recalls a very important formula of the Divine Circle from Dante's *Vita Nuova* (12.4): "Ego tanquam centrum circuli, cui simili modo se habent circumferentie partes" (I am as the center of a circle, to which the parts of the circumference have a similar relation). These words, spoken by Amor, are variously interpreted, but all interpretations agree that the geometrical scheme here is the pattern of inner harmony and moral perfection. It is a moral implication of the cosmological model.[9] It is notable that the other famous thinker who expanded speculation about the center and periphery of a circle into theology and cosmology—thereby considerably affecting the transformation of the medieval universe into that of modernity—was Nicholas of Cusa. He wrote that "the Machine of the World" has its center everywhere and its circle nowhere, "for its circle and center is God, Who is everywhere and nowhere."[10] While Nicholas, like Dante, uses this model to justify a parallelism between natural and supernatural, Nicholas did not regard the model as providing a stable and hierarchical structure for the universe, instead believing that it revealed the universe's relativity. He speaks about a circle whose center is everywhere and nowhere, while arguing that the Earth is not the stable center of the universe. His ideas about the motion of Earth and sun, the infinity of the universe, and the possible inhabitants of stars and planets, anticipated and even partly outstripped Copernicus's discoveries. The image of the "Machine" is remarkable here in the light of the later Cartesian mechanicism.

Nicholas of Cusa, the first thinker to teach the homogeneity of the sublunar sphere and heavenly spheres, of Earth and stars, directs us to the last—philosophical—variation of the center and rim leitmotif in Lewis's corpus, found in the latter's declarative "Science-Fiction Cradlesong." It is notable that Lewis initially published this poem under the title "Cradle-Song Based on a Theme from Nicholas of Cusa." This is one more illustration of the peculiar alliance of science fiction and theology in the thought of the author of *Perelandra*.

By and by Man will try
To get out into the sky,
Sailing far beyond the air
From Down and Here to Up and There.
Stars and sky, sky and stars
Make us feel the prison bars.

Suppose it done. Now we ride
Closed in steel, up there, outside;
Through our port-holes see the vast
Heaven-scape go rushing past.
Shall we? All that meets the eye
Is sky and stars, stars and sky.

Points of light with black between
Hang like a painted scene
Motionless, no nearer there
Than on Earth, everywhere
Equidistant from our ship.
Heaven has given us the slip.

Hush, be still. Outer space
Is a concept, not a place.
Try no more. Where we are

Never can be sky or star.
From prison, in a prison, we fly;
There's no way into the sky.[11]

Here we have an instance of true apophaticism or, to use Charles Williams's terminology, the Way of Rejection of images.[12] In an era in which mankind dreamed of the cosmos (the poem was written in 1954), Lewis broke his own image of bright heavens and inverted the construction once more. Now substantially imprisoned, floating in black and motionless space, man is the center of a universe, "everywhere equidistant from our ship." But it is a dead center, a philosophical version of Dante's "Luciferocentrical" construction. Man is not—as in *Perelandra*—a governor of Creation; it does not incline to him but escapes him. In several half-playful lines, Lewis concentrates his fundamental idea: Human progress, if it does not presuppose an extreme inner transfiguration, is doomed to "drop Heaven upon itself." The longing to "get *out* into the sky," to move "from Down and Here to Up and There" misses the direction. "Outer space / Is a concept, not a place": The bent mind cannot escape its prison spatially, but only morally, having learned to see the Heavens as *inner* space. This is a good occasion to recall the directional motto of Narnia: "further up and further in"—from the periphery to the center. The "theme from Nicholas of Cusa" mentioned in the poem's title may be the above-mentioned cosmological speculation from the second book of *Docta Ignorantia;* however, Thomas Amos sagely points out another less obvious, but very interesting, parallel,[13] from Nicholas of Cusa's *De visione Dei* 9:

> I experience the necessity for me to enter into obscuring mist and to admit the coincidence of opposites, beyond all capacity of reason, and to seek truth where impossibility appears. And when—beyond that [rational capacity] and beyond every most lofty intellectual ascent, as well—I come to that which is unknown to every intellect and which every intellect judges to be very far removed from the truth, *there* You are present, my God. . . . And I have found the abode wherein You dwell unveiledly—an abode surrounded by the coincidence of contradictories. And [this coincidence] is the wall of Paradise, wherein You dwell. The gate of this wall is guarded by a most lofty rational spirit; unless this spirit is vanquished the entrance will not be

accessible. Therefore, on the *other* side of the coincidence of contradictories You can be seen—but not at all on this side.[14]

This fragment finds many parallels in Lewis's writings, the description of the wall of the Garden of Love in *The Allegory of Love* being only the most obvious. Being, like Williams, an enthusiast of the way of affirmation of images, Lewis was also fully aware of its shortcomings. Like Andreas Capellanus, one of the personages of *The Allegory of Love*, Lewis supplied his highly imaginative writings with some important palinodes, or retracting statements; examples include his essay "Christianity and Culture," with its declaration of the auxiliary character of culture, and, particularly, *A Grief Observed*, with its motif of God as "the great iconoclast."[15] *The Discarded Image* ends in the same way. The medieval image of the world, which Lewis confessedly prefers to the modern one, is irreversibly discarded. But instead of it we have not a new image but the understanding that all of them are only images, merely pointing to the *realissima.*

Thus, the "heavenly" pages of *The Discarded Image* can make a very prolific context for analysis of the center and the rim motif in *Perelandra*. Having outlined this motif in the Cosmic Trilogy both mystically and in terms of science fiction, Lewis explored it philosophically in poetry and scientifically in *The Discarded Image*. An appetence to the Heavens, as to the realm of unbent nature and moral patterns, was customary for European scientists, philosophers, and mystics from the very beginning of European tradition. In Lewis we find, characteristically, the urgency of joyful disappointment, of the happy inversion or eucatastrophe, when the *Weltanschauung* of modernity collides with the medieval one, forcing the spectator to leave his or her stable position. Thus we can see familiar things and ideas as strange, which is one of the most important characteristics of Lewis's method. As "Cradle-song" reminds us, it is impossible—or fruitless—to deal with such things as models of the universe merely *in abstracto;* using them requires self-involvement and a kind of moral endeavor. To see the real center, you should just cease pretending to be the center yourself, a feeling the more impressive the less it is perceived in material reality.

Notes

1. "His works are all of a piece: a book in one genre will correct, illuminate, or amplify what is latent in another. Hence the opening chapters of the *Allegory* must now be read in the light of the closing pages of *The Four Loves*—where he retracts his view that passionate love was largely a literary phenomenon; whilst those same pages lead us straight to the first theme of *The Discarded Image*—namely, the appearance of pagan, or neoplatonic elements in the formative writers of the medieval Christian tradition. The Merlin who in a very literal sense underlies the action of *That Hideous Strength* is the Merlin who was to figure in his selections from Layamon's *Brut*. And in *Till We Have Faces* the expositor of allegory himself writes an allegory so haunting and so suggestive that it makes Fulgentius's allegorical interpretation of this tale of Cupid and Psyche seem strained and Boccaccio's gloss on it merely mechanical." J. A. W. Bennett, *The Humane Medievalist: An Inaugural Lecture* (Cambridge, UK: Cambridge Univ. Press, 1965), 27.

2. C. S. Lewis, *P* (New York: Simon and Schuster, 1996), 213–14.

3. In *The Discarded Image*, Lewis notes that it was Milton who introduced the term *space* in its modern Newtonian meaning; see C. S. Lewis, *DI* (Cambridge, UK: Cambridge Univ. Press, 1994), 100.

4. In Lewis's *Allegory of Love*, we find the following excellent fragment from Alain de Lille's *De Planctu Naturae:*

> Consider, quoth she [Nature], how in this world, as in some noble city, Reason is set up and established by the measurable governance of the commonweal's majesty. In Heaven, as in the castle of an earthly city, the eternal Emperor eternally hath his throne, from whom eternally goeth forth his edict that the notions of things single be written in the book of his providence. In the Air, that is, in the middle parts of the city, there liveth in arms an heavenly host of angels, the which with delegated service doth diligently exercise its watch over men. And man, truly, as an alien that dwelleth without the city wall, refuseth not his obedience to those angelic knights. Therefore in this commonweal God commandeth, the angel operateth, and man obeyeth. God by commandment maketh man, the angel by operation bringeth him to being, the man by obedience remaketh himself again . . . of the which right ordinate commonweal the likeness is within man also reflected. In the castle of whose head Sapience sitteth and is at rest as an empress, unto whom, as to a goddess, the residue of his powers as half-goddesses do obey. For his power of engin, and his force logical, and his virtue memorial of things passed, having their habitations in divers chambers of his head, are ever busied about their obedience to her. In the heart, forsooth, that is, in the middle parts of the city, Magnanimity hath her house; who having received the order of knighthood under the reign

of Wisdom, doth by operation fulfil whatsoever things that governance deliberateth. But the reins, which is as much as to say the parts without the wall, permit a dwelling in the uttermost region of the body to lustful pleasures, which serve the will of Magnanimity, neither dare they set themselves against her commandment. Therefore in this commonweal, Sapience beareth the part of the one commanding, Magnanimity hath the likeness of one operating, Lust showeth the image of one obeying.

Alain de Lille, *De Planctu Naturae*, Prosa III , in *The Anglo-Latin Satirical Poets and Epigrammatists of the Twelfth Century*, ed. Thomas Wright (London: Longman and Co., 1872), 2:429–522, quoted in Lewis, *AOL* (London: Oxford Univ. Press, 1938), 108–9; Lewis's translation.

5. Dante, *Paradiso* 28.25–39, in *The Comedy of Dante Alighieri, the Florentine: Paradise*, trans. Barbara Reynolds (Harmondsworth, Middlesex: Penguin, 1962):

> distante intorno al punto un cerchio d'igne
> si girava sì ratto, ch'avria vinto
> quel moto che più tosto il mondo cigne;
>
> e questo era d'un altro circumcinto,
> e quel dal terzo, e 'l terzo poi dal quarto,
> dal quinto il quarto, e poi dal sesto il quinto.
>
> Sopra seguiva il settimo sì sparto
> già di larghezza, che 'l messo di Iuno
> intero a contenerlo sarebbe arto.
>
> Così l'ottavo e 'l nono; e chiascheduno
> più tardo si movea, secondo ch'era
> in numero distante più da l'uno;
>
> e quello avea la fiamma più sincera
> cui men distava la favilla pura,
> credo, però che più di lei s'invera.

6. Cf. C. S. Lewis, *LB* (1956; New York: HarperCollins, 1984), 207:

> "The further up and further in you go, the bigger everything gets. The inside is larger than the outside."
>
> Lucy looked hard at the garden and saw that it was not really a garden at all but a whole world, with its own rivers and woods and sea and mountains. But they were not strange: she knew them all.
>
> "I see," she said, "this is still Narnia, and more real and more beautiful than the Narnia down below. . . . I see . . . world within world, Narnia within Narnia."
>
> "Yes," said Mr. Tumnus, "like an onion: except that as you continue to go in and in, each circle is larger than the last."

7. Eucatastrophe is a usual device employed by Lewis to express a meeting with *Joy.* Ransom is brought to Mars by deceit; by deceit Uncle Andrew, in *The Magician's Nephew,* sends Polly and Digory to the other world (one of many examples in the Narnia books); and with such eucatastrophe ends *Till We Have Faces.*

8. C. S. Lewis, *OSP* (New York: Macmillan, 1968), 32. The epilogue of Milton's *Comus,* which Lewis quotes in the final lines of the fragment, is very interesting in the context of our theme:

The dances ended, the Spirit epiloguizes:
To the ocean now I fly,
And those happy climes that lie
Where day never shuts his eye,
Up in the broad fields of the sky.
There I suck the liquid air,
All amidst the gardens fair
Of Hesperus, and his daughters three
That sing about the golden tree.
Along the crisped shades and bowers
Revels the spruce and jocund Spring;
The Graces and the rosy-bosomed Hours
Thither all their bounties bring.
There eternal Summer dwells;
And west winds with musky wing
About the cedarn alleys fling
Nard and cassia's balmy smells.
Iris there with humid bow
Waters the odorous banks, that blow
Flowers of more mingled hue
Than her purfled scarf can shew,
And drenches with Elysian dew
(List, mortals, if your ears be true)
Beds of hyacinth and roses,
Where young Adonis oft reposes,
Waxing well of his deep wound,
In slumber soft, and on the ground
Sadly sits the Assyrian queen.
But far above, in spangled sheen,
Celestial Cupid, her famed son, advanced
Holds his dear Psyche, sweet entranced
After her wandering labours long,
Till free consent the gods among
Make her his eternal bride,
And from her fair unspotted side

Two blissful twins are to be born,
Youth and Joy; so Jove hath sworn.
But now my task is smoothly done:
I can fly, or I can run,
Quickly to the green earth's end,
Where the bowed welkin slow doth bend,
And from thence can soar as soon
To the corners of the moon.
Mortals, that would follow me,
Love virtue; she alone is free.
She can teach ye how to climb
Higher than the sphery chime;
Or, if Virtue feeble were,
Heaven itself would stoop to her.

John Milton, *Comus*, 976–1023. See *The English Poems of John Milton*, ed. R. C. Browne (Oxford: Clarendon Press, 1877), 35–36.

9. A representative survey of interpretations is found in Dante Alighieri, *Vita Nuova*, ed. Marcello Ciccuto (Milan: BUR, 2004), 127–28.

10. Nicholas of Cusa, *De docta ignorantia*, 2.12.

11. C. S. Lewis, "Cradle-Song Based on a Theme from Nicholas of Cusa," *Times Literary Supplement*, June 11, 1954, 375; rpt. as "Science-Fiction Cradlesong" in Lewis, *Poems*, ed. Walter Hooper (New York: Harcourt, Brace & World, 1967), 57–58. (This is not to be confused with the poem "On Another Theme from Nicholas of Cusa," *The Times Literary Supplement*, Jan. 21, 1955, 43; rpt. in revised form as "On a Theme from Nicholas of Cusa [*De Docta Ignorantia*, III. ix]" in *Poems*, 70.)

12. See Charles Williams, *The Figure of Beatrice: A Study in Dante* (1943; London: D. S. Brewer, 1994), 8ff.

13. Thomas Amos, "There's No Way into the Sky," *Inklings-Jahrbuch* 19 (2001): 237–41.

14. Nicholas of Cusa, *Nicholas of Cusa's Dialectical Mysticism: Text, Translation, and Interpretive Study of* De Visione Dei, ed. and trans. Jasper Hopkins, 3rd ed. (Minneapolis, Minn.: Arthur J. Banning Press, 2007), 697.

15. C. S. Lewis, "Christianity and Culture," in Lewis, *CR* (Grand Rapids, Mich.: Wm. B. Eermans Publishing, 1994), 12–36; C. S. Lewis, *AGO* (New York: Bantam, 1983), 76–77.

Morality and Meaning

in

Perelandra

Perelandran Diction

A Study in Meaning

TAMI VAN OPSTAL

Though many students of literature need no introduction to the works of C. S. Lewis, few would profess any familiarity with "the wisest and best of [his] unofficial teachers." Lewis not only praises Owen Barfield in these words in his dedication to *The Allegory of Love* but elsewhere explicitly recommends Barfield's book *Poetic Diction* to his readers. This paper explores the extent of Barfield's influence upon Lewis's *Perelandra,* first reviewing Barfield's theory of language and meaning, as set forth in *Poetic Diction* and other works, and then studying the characters of the Green Lady, Ransom, and Weston with an eye to Barfield's thesis.

OWEN BARFIELD ON WORDS, CONSCIOUSNESS, AND MEANING

It was at a tea in 1919 that C. S. Lewis first met Owen Barfield, beginning a friendship that would last the rest of Lewis's life. In the 1930s, Barfield became an original member of the Inklings, the informal Oxford literary group to which Lewis also belonged, and his ideas often became central preoccupations of the group.[1] However, Lewis and Barfield had philosophical exchanges long before the Inklings ever met at the Eagle and Child. Perhaps the most contentious of their dialogues, the series of letters Lewis named "The Great War," began in 1925 and dealt both with Barfield's anthroposophist beliefs and with the thesis of Barfield's book,

Poetic Diction. These exchanges refined and enriched Barfield's arguments, and when *Poetic Diction* was finally published in 1928, he acknowledged the importance of Lewis's thoughts on his project by dedicating the book to him with an epigraph by William Blake, "Opposition is true friendship." While Lewis clearly rejected anthroposophy, what Owen Barfield taught Lewis did have a reverberating impact on Lewis; as Lionel Adey writes in *C. S. Lewis's "Great War" with Owen Barfield,* "[One] would need a close acquaintance with Lewis's published and unpublished writings to realize how the thesis marshaled Lewis's thoughts the way they were going."[2]

The title of Barfield's dissertation, *Poetic Diction,* may give readers the misleading impression that the book is a study of the aesthetic and technical aspects of good poetry, which Barfield's argument does indeed treat. However, it is the book's subtitle, *A Study in Meaning,* that hints at the more ambitious thesis of Barfield's work, which is nothing less than a comprehensive theory of language and meaning and of the historical development of language and words. In articulating this theory, Barfield introduces new ideas about the relationship of metaphor and meaning, the evolution of human consciousness, and the importance of poetry and imagination.

According to Barfield, all language is metaphorical; it is through metaphor that humans gain knowledge. Early in *Poetic Diction,* Barfield defines metaphor as the enabling recognition of the "resemblances" and "analogies" that give us knowledge, and he asserts that "all *meaning*—even the most primitive kind—is dependent on the possession of some measure of this power" of metaphor-making.[3] The average word, he claims, is a petrified metaphor, a once-fresh recognition of a relationship between two things, which has become so tired through common use that we forget that it was ever new or alive. "Whatever word we hit on," Barfield explains, "if we trace its meaning far enough back, we find it apparently expressive of some tangible, or at all events perceptible object or some physical activity."[4] One example Barfield cites of the power of metaphor is the poet Shelley's statement that the "soul is an enchanted boat." Barfield proposes that this metaphor might become so explicit a connection as to produce a new word, *chambote,* for "soul." In fact, he asserts, most words are born this way. It would not be long, however, before people used *chambote* for "soul" without recognizing the rich metaphor that created the word. This is an illustration of the way metaphor transforms "simple perceptual meanings" into new words and eventually abstractions, for as the metaphor solidifies into a new word the connotation recedes farther from the concrete object or activity that gave it its name.[5] Barfield does not argue that meaning evolves through metaphor or that the maker of metaphor is also the creator of meaning; instead, he contends that "poetic and *apparently* 'metaphorical' values were latent in meaning from the beginning."[6] When Shelley compares the soul to an enchanted boat, he is not himself creating the attribute of the soul that is dreamlike and magical; rather, he is merely articulating the quality he recognizes as already existing in reality. "Ancient man," writes Barfield, "neither invented the gods nor projected human feelings into a meaningless cosmos, but expressed a life and meaning inherent in nature";[7] such ancients recognized the connectedness and unity of meaning, and their languages thus reflected the "old, concrete, *undivided* meaning." To explain this idea, Barfield gives the example of the Latin word *spiritus*, which means not only "blowing" and "wind," but also "breath of the mouth," "life," and "the spiritual element in man." Barfield asserts that these various meanings are not merely metaphorical, a recognition by an ancient poet that wind, breath, life, and spirit share the same qualities; they are an acknowledgment and expression of an essentially connected and indivisible reality. Another example comes from mythology, which can be thought of as metaphor on a larger scale: the story of Demeter, whose daughter Persephone is stolen away to the underworld by Hades and whose sadness causes winter. Barfield makes the argument that this myth and other myths, contrary to popular opinion, were not the constructs of prescientific philosophers attempting to *explain* natural phenomena. Instead, these myths were intended to communicate one "all pervasive meaning" or self-evident connection among phenomena such as "death and sleep and winter." Now, however, "mythology is the ghost of concrete meaning. Connections, which are now apprehended as metaphor, were once perceived as immediate realities."[8]

According to Barfield, mythology and metaphors are "ghostly" because language experienced a sort of fall, a severing of connections and separation from the truth of unified meaning. While the language of the ancients was concrete and rich in meaning, modern languages are abstract. In *Saving the Appearances*, Barfield claims that the shift from the concrete to the abstract was the "'polarization' of an ancient unity into an outer and an inner meaning."[9] The immaterial and material meanings are now divorced. A demonstration of this separation of meanings is found in

Barfield's book, *Speaker's Meaning,* and is a comparison of the original Greek and the English translation of the Gospel of John 3:6–8. In English these verses read:

> 6. That which is born of the flesh is flesh; and that which is born of the spirit is spirit.
> 7. Marvel not that I said unto thee, Ye must be born again.
> 8. The wind bloweth where it listeth, and thou hearest the sound thereof, but canst not tell whence it cometh, and whither it goeth: so is everyone that is born of the spirit.[10]

The Greek version, however, uses the same word, *pneuma,* for "spirit," and "wind." According to Barfield, "the English translators had to split it into two words" to convey both the inner and outer meanings contained together in the one Greek word.[11] According to Barfield, the evolution of consciousness made this sort of splitting up of concrete and abstract, or inner and outer meanings necessary.

Barfield's theory of language is inextricably entwined with his theory about the evolution of consciousness, and because it is impossible to understand one without the other, it is important to familiarize oneself with his vocabulary and his arguments. In many of his books, Barfield speaks of human consciousness in terms of "participation," his term for the way in which either individual or collective minds take part in the "universal mind,"[12] or "the extra-sensory relation between man and the phenomena."[13] Barfield believed that the earliest humans had what he calls "original participation," something much closer to the way animals interact with nature, an *experiential* rather than theoretical relationship with it. In *Poetic Diction,* Barfield speaks of participation in terms of being able to recognize the true relationships between objects, phenomena, and actions and their immaterial meanings; while the ancient mind observed the unity of meanings through "direct perceptual experience," the development of human consciousness has left men without the power to see the one meaning as one.[14]

The incapacity to see unified meaning springs from the rational principle and, more specifically, the scientific mind-set, which involves dissection and distinction and has inexorably separated concrete from abstract meaning. Lionel Adey explains that eventually "discursive intellect forever dries up meanings" and fossilizes metaphorical connections.[15] According to Barfield, while the ancients had naturally poetic minds and "participant knowledge," a perception that hardly even separated the object under observation from the observer, our minds are logical and our perception dominated by "scientific understanding." Now, the rational principle "shuts off the human ego from the living meaning in the outer world . . . and encloses that ego in the network of its own, now abstract thoughts." Therefore, as the connections among objects, phenomena, and meaning have been separated, so have humans been separated from nature. The rational principle has made men self-conscious. This is the story Barfield tells of the development of human consciousness and its attack on unified meaning. The relationships between concrete and abstract meanings, the ancient unities, still exist "independently, not indeed of Thought, but of any individual thinker." They are not subjective, but they have been lost and forgotten: "like sleeping beauties, they lie there prone and rigid in the walls of Castle Logic, waiting only for the kiss of metaphor to awaken them to fresh life." Barfield concludes that the only remedy for abstraction and the dividing of meanings is "that experience of truth or identification of the self with the meaning of Life, which is both poetry and knowledge."[16]

After the beginning of the rational age, then, metaphor and poetry have the power to rediscover meaning, granting the poet a special role. "Every object has some relationship to every other, and every metaphor exposes a patch of connective tissue."[17] "Poets," asserts Barfield, "through creation of true metaphors, *restore* the unity which has been forgotten." There are true and untrue metaphors, then, because the relations between objects are not invented by men, but exist independently in reality: "Every metaphor is 'true' only in so far as it contains such a reality."[18] Barfield proposes that true metaphors mark a restoration of the unity of the subject and object, for a "true, imaginative metaphor . . . expresses and may communicate participant knowledge." Ancient poets were considered to be divinely inspired by the Muses because of their ability to intuit relationships and create metaphors; for us, now, Barfield argues, they act as comparers, judges, and even life-givers, as they restore the meaning of words. Language, then, "is the storehouse of imagination" where the metaphors of poets are fossilized and absorbed into the consciousness of a people.[19]

Barfield did not believe that humans could ever return to a state of original participation, or even that it would be good if they could; rather, he argued that through acquaintance with the source of life, humans can arrive at *final* participation, or a conscious and willing identification with the meaning of life. In *Saving the Appearances*, Barfield connects final participation and the renewal of meaning in language with the Incarnation of Christ, the Word in flesh: "If we meditated deeply enough on the nature and development of meaning in language—we could, if necessary, infer without other help, that the turning-point of time must have occurred. We could infer that the incarnation of the Word must have culminated." In doing so, Barfield also associates the fall of man with the fall of language, the loss of original participation: "We have seen how original participation, which began as the unconscious identity of man with his Creator, shrank, as his self-consciousness increased, and how this was associated with the origin and development of language." Separation from true unified meaning corresponds with human alienation from God. This disunity began to be resolved when "in one man the inwardness of the Divine Name had been fully realized; the final participation, whereby man's Creator speaks from within man himself, had been accomplished. The Word had been made flesh." Christ's coming, in other words, makes it possible for all men to transition between original and final participation, for "since the death and resurrection—the heart is fired from within by the Christ."[20]

It is important at this point to emphasize that as much as Lewis may have come to agree generally with Barfield's thesis on language, meaning, and metaphor, he in a sense corrects and "christens" those aspects of Barfield's thought that prove incompatible with orthodoxy. While Barfield borrows words and phrases from orthodox Christianity, he, as an anthroposophist, often does not mean the same thing by them. For instance, Barfield describes "participation" both as identification with the Creator and as unity with the collective consciousness or "universal mind";[21] Barfield, that is, considers man to participate in a fundamental spiritual unity with God, the Divine Word. Orthodox Christianity, in contrast, teaches that God as Creator is wholly other and distinct from his creation as well as from the creatures he made, even though, according to the Bible, "from him and through him and to him are all things."[22] For Lewis, then, "final participation" means the conscious *communion* of man with his Creator rather than their spiritual and mental *unity* of consciousness. In addition, Barfield believes that the Incarnation was a pivotal event because it paved the way to final participation through the evolution of consciousness, not because it was God's provision for renewed relationship with his creation.

Edwin Woodruff Tait provides some helpful further explanation of the divergences between Lewis and Barfield's beliefs in his essay, "Owen Barfield: Un-Regressed Pilgrim": While Barfield could compare the loss of participation to the sin of Adam, they are not the same thing. The former occurs relatively late in human history and can be transcended by the evolution of consciousness. The Fall of Adam as Lewis and orthodox Christianity understand it occurs at the beginning of human history, is located in the will more fundamentally than in the intellect, and can be overcome not through evolution but only through repentance and return."[23] That is, while for Lewis the Fall has alienated man from God and corrupts his nature, so that he cannot return to him except by God's grace through Jesus Christ, Barfield uses the term *the Fall* to signify the tragedy that occurred on the road to self-consciousness of man's fundamental unity with God. Christ is significant as the realization of this unity of God and man, not as the propitiation for sin.

These differences are of such theological consequence for a Christian that one might be inclined to reject the idea that Barfield could have had considerable influence on the thought of a Christian writer such as C. S. Lewis. This rejection, however, would deny the debt Lewis personally acknowledged to Barfield. In the following argument, I will attempt to show more particularly the significant, even profound, influence Barfield can be seen to have had on Lewis, especially in *Perelandra*. In order to do so, I will at times use Barfield's terms; however, I will use them in the context of Lewis's "christening" of Barfield's theory.

BARFIELD IN SPACE: LANGUAGE, UNITY, AND CONSCIOUSNESS ON *PERELANDRA*

"May I ask you, Dr. Ransom, what is the meaning of this?"
—Dr. Weston, in C. S. Lewis, *Perelandra*

In 1936, a few years after C. S. Lewis's conversion to Christianity, Barfield tried to prod Lewis into renewing hostilities and restarting the "Great War." Lewis responded, "When a truth has ceased to be a mistress for pleasure, and become a wife for fruit it is almost unnatural to go back to the dialectic ardours of the wooing."[24] What he gained through the ardors of discussion with Owen Barfield certainly became fruitful for Lewis in the years to come, incorporating itself into much of his fiction. Published between 1938 and 1945, more than fifteen years after the end of the "Great War," Lewis's Ransom Trilogy, so-called for its protagonist, Elwin Ransom, includes *Out of the Silent Planet,* which takes Ransom to Mars, *Perelandra,* in which he visits Venus, and *That Hideous Strength,* which returns the story to Earth and Oxford. According to Gregory Wolfe, the unifying theme of the trilogy is language, and the first hint of this theme for an observant reader is the profession of the good Dr. Ransom, who is a philologist, a lover of language.[25] While all three books share a preoccupation with language and reflect Owen Barfield's thesis on language and meaning, *Perelandra* most clearly embodies the connectedness of Lewis and Barfield's thought and reveals the extent to which Barfield's work became wedded to Lewis's imagination.

In *Perelandra,* Ransom recognizes the brokenness of the language of fallen humans and struggles with the resultant barriers to meaningful communication. The Green Lady is accustomed to perfect communication and unified meaning, and Weston attempts to destroy both and introduce sin by manipulating language. These different dispositions toward language and meaning hint at deeper differences between the characters, and the growth of consciousness of the Green Lady, Ransom, and Weston corresponds with stages of Barfield's theory of language, portraying in different ways its inseparability from the development of consciousness.

THE GREEN LADY

The Green Lady, the unfallen human inhabitant of Perelandra, can be seen as a portrait of the prerational human of Barfield's theory. Many characteristics that Owen Barfield attributes to pagan or ancient man are present in her language, person, and consciousness. For Barfield, *ancient* is a loaded term, referring to the first period in the development of human language, the period when language reflected the connectedness and unity of meaning in the world. The Green Lady, being one of the two first humans on Venus, speaks the same "ancient language" spoken on Malacandra, also called Old Solar; however, Ransom notices that the Green Lady herself is in such close communion with Maledil that she does not even need speech or language to experience unbroken, meaningful communication with him. Without being told by Ransom and with no other way of learning, she knows about and describes the Sorns of Malacandra and various features of the Malacandran landscape. When Ransom asks how she knew, she says simply, "It all comes into my mind now"; that is, Maledil has revealed it to her. Later, the Green Lady wants to scrape her knee as an experiment, curious to learn what Ransom means by "pain," a sensation she has never experienced; yet Ransom concludes that "Maledil apparently told her not to," directly commanding her not to harm herself.[26] This episode not only displays the communion of the Green Lady with Maledil, it also typifies her inability to grasp merely abstract meaning apart from the concrete, such as an encounter with pain. On Perelandra, communication is so unfettered that speech is sometimes superfluous.

The Green Lady's own use of language is concrete and metaphorical. When she encounters something new, her first reaction is to connect it to something concrete she already knows. Instances of this include her asking Ransom about the "little hills and valleys" that appear in his forehead when he is confused, naming the half-sunburned Ransom after ridiculous, harlequinlike animals called "piebalds," and dismissing a meaningless statement as a "tree without fruit." This linkage to the concrete is also evident in her struggle to understand desire. The concept of wishing for or wanting something more or other than what she has initially confuses the Green Lady; she lives with such obedience in God's will that she would never think to be discontented or disappointed. However, her conversations with Ransom introduce her to the idea of desire, and she finds a meaningful expression for expectation in a concrete metaphor: "One goes into the forest to pick fruit and already the thought of one fruit rather than another has grown up in one's mind. Then, it may be, one finds a different fruit and not the fruit one thought of. One joy was expected and another is given."[27] Her world is meaningful and unified; she even translates Ransom's abstract terms back into concrete and living terms.

In the Green Lady, Lewis also synthesizes Owen Barfield's theory of prerational consciousness and original participation with the biblical portrayal of the first humans' communion with God and with nature. In several places, Barfield describes original participation as similar in some ways to the consciousness of animals, which have a close, experiential relationship with nature; indeed, when Ransom relates his first observations of the Green Lady, he remarks that she seems to possess the "purity and peace of an animal." Her life is one of immediacy, lived moment by moment, so when Ransom tries to explain the idea of time to her, she is at first confused, then responds, "I have never done it before—stepping out of life into the Alongside and looking at oneself living as if one were not alive." This "alongside world" of thought about oneself—this splitting of herself into subject and object—is so completely new to her that she realizes that she was previously unaware of the autonomy of her own will. "I have been so young till this moment," she remarks, "that all my life now seems to have been a kind of sleep. I have thought that I was being carried, and behold, I was walking."[28] Like Barfield's pagan, who has such a close, experiential relationship with nature that he is unaware of his separateness from his world, the Green Lady is unaware of her own individuality both in relation to nature and to God.

This realization of her own consciousness is the first step in the Green Lady's movement from original to final participation. Up until this point, she has lived in such close connection with the source of life, following wherever Maledil leads, that she did not even know that she had chosen to obey his will by floating with the islands wherever they took her, caring for the animals of the planet—animals which in turn obey her as she does God—eating whatever fruit Maledil provided, and embracing without hesitation even separation from the King, her husband. Again, she is amazed at her selfhood when she exclaims, "I thought . . . that I was carried in the will of Him I love, but now I see that I walk with it." She is stunned at this recognition and asks, "How has He made me so separate from Himself?" As the Green Lady learns about her own "separateness" from God, it teaches her more about the richness of obedience; however, as Ransom notices when he first starts introducing the Green Lady to new ideas, there is a "precariousness" to the consciousness of the woman as she learns more about herself.[29] In *Saving the Appearances*, Barfield says that for humans, original participation "began as the unconscious identity of man with his Creator" and that it "shrank, as his self-consciousness increased."[30] Like the humans of Thulcandra, or Earth, the woman is in danger of losing her communion with God as she becomes more self-aware. Her consciousness is imperiled by the arrival on Perelandra of Weston, the progressive scientist whose desire to conquer space for the preservation of mankind took both him and Ransom into space for the first time in *Out of the Silent*

Planet. While Ransom desires to preserve the Green Lady's relationship with God, Weston acts as her tempter, coming to introduce her to pain, to give her "death in abundance," and to separate her from Maledil and life.[31] In Weston's (or the Un-man's) conversations with the Green Lady, he tries to direct her further inward in order to sever her dependence on God, since she must first know that she possesses a will independent of God's will before she can assert that will against God's.

A large part of Weston's temptation of the woman involves killing words, making them mean nothing, especially through his manipulation of stories and poetry and his creation of an "alongside world" of what might be, rather than what is (*P,* 104). Instead of faithfully representing truth and reality with his words and his stories, he uses them to distort truth. He tells the Green Lady that the women of Earth are made beautiful by tragedy and pain and that they are powerful in their independence. As she entertains his arguments, the Green Lady responds, "Your words are like no other words that I have ever heard. . . . They make me think of—of—I do not know what they make me think of" (*P,* 114). At first, she is at pains to find a metaphor, and cannot, because there is no truth and no meaning in what he says. Yet she entertains his arguments, and, as a result, "fondles the idea of disobedience" (*P,* 131). Ransom pleads with her, "Can you not see that he is making you say words that mean nothing?" (*P,* 132). Weston, now the Un-Man, tells her that God would be pleased if she asserted her will and became more fully "her own," and frustrated, she exclaims: "Fruit without taste! How can I step out of His will save into something that cannot be wished? . . . It would be like trying to walk on water or swim through islands. . . . I thought your words had a meaning. But now it seems they have none. To walk out of His will is to walk into nowhere" (*P,* 115).

At the end of her ordeal, having undergone and overcome the temptation of the Un-Man, the Green Lady has achieved an increased knowledge of her own will and, therefore, a richer understanding of submission of that will to Maledil. What had been blind obedience is transformed into the fullest communion, or final participation, because of a change in the Green Lady's self-consciousness. In *Saving the Appearances,* Barfield states, "Logically, there was the possibility of a gentle, untragic transition from original to final participation, the one maturing in proportion as the other faded."[32] This sort of transition did not take place on Earth, but, in the Green Lady, Lewis gives us a picture of how this could have happened. Because she has matured through an awareness of her own will, she is able to submit more completely to the will of Maledil, and a great change takes place in Perelandra. Malacandra, the ruler of the planet Mars, explains to Ransom: "To-day for the first time two creatures of the low worlds, two images of Maledil that breathe and breed like the beasts, step up that step at which your parents fell, and sit in the throne of what they were meant to be," more completely like their Creator (*P,* 197).

As the Green Lady and her husband the King are crowned, Perelandra, the angelic being who has ruled the planet until now, turns over to them all authority over that world, saying, "My word henceforth is nothing: your word is law unchangeable and the very daughter of the Voice. . . . Enjoy it well. Give names to all creatures, guide all natures to perfection" (*P,* 206). Because they are now even more fully unified with God, their words carry with them his authority. As the Green Lady and the King start naming places and animals on the planet, it is clear that they are speaking the names God has given them to speak. Their ability to name things—to see and speak meaning—comes directly from their communion with God. Earlier in the book, Ransom had predicted that an increase in the woman's consciousness could actually increase her participation with God if only that self-consciousness could be prevented from causing her fall into self-will: "Certainly it must be part of the Divine plan that this happy creature should mature, should become more and more a creature of free choice, should become, in a sense, more distinct from God and from her husband in order thereby to be at one with them in a richer fashion . . . an obedience freer, more reasoned, more conscious than any she had known before, was being put in her power" (*P,* 133).

The Green Lady's increase in self-consciousness does indeed lead to final participation, this "freer, more reasoned, more conscious" obedience, and to a closer communion with nature, her husband, and God because now she willingly participates in the will of God. This richer participation leads to an increase in authority over Perelandra, even the authority to make new words and names, to make words that carry with them the weight of an enactment.

RANSOM

Ransom is, as has been said, a philologist, and his conclusions about language during his time in *Perelandra* echo Barfield's story of the fall of language and the redemption of meaning through contact with the source of Life. Upon arriving on Perelandra, Ransom expresses frustration that words simply cannot express what he sees and experiences. The inadequacy of words, as well as Ransom's interactions with the Green Lady, leads him to conclude that the language of Earth itself is flawed and fallen. Finding that the Green Lady speaks Old Solar, the same language spoken by the inhabitants of Malacandra, confirms Ransom's belief that "there was originally a common speech for all rational creatures inhabiting the planets of our system. That original speech was lost on Thulcandra, our own world, when our tragedy took place. No human language now known in the world is descended from it" (*P,* 25).

The "tragedy," mankind's Fall into sin, also damaged his ability to communicate. As a result, the Green Lady, who has no conception of sin, often has difficulty understanding Ransom, even though he speaks to her in Old Solar. Broken humans speak in a broken language, since enshrined and perpetuated in human language are the broken concepts of fallen human beings. The perfect communion the Green Lady experiences with Maledil makes the faultiness of Ransom's communication even more frustrating.

Because human communication is fallen and insufficient, it is in danger of being meaningless. As noted before, at one point in one of their conversations, Ransom, perplexed and showing his confusion, wrinkles his forehead. The Green Lady asks him, "Why, O Piebald, are you making little hills and valleys in your forehead . . . Are those signs of something in your world?" Ransom replies, "They mean nothing," but immediately feels guilty for his lie and for his denial of meaning (*P,* 70). Up to this point, the Green Lady assumes a meaning behind his every word and action, but after this point, she is repeatedly perplexed and put off by meaningless statements. For example, during another conversation Ransom explains that "in our world, when they say a man talks much they mean they wish him to be silent," and the Green Lady asks, "If that is what they mean, why do they not say it?" Later in this conversation, she accuses Ransom: "you had nothing to say about it and yet made the nothing up into words" (*P,* 75). Indeed, the lady has a favorite metaphor for words and sayings that mean nothing to her:

they are "like a tree with no fruit" (*P,* 105). To her, human language has all the signs of life, like a tree, but it falls short of its purpose of communication and is in danger of being fruitless or meaningless.

The trajectory of Ransom's consciousness also reflects a Barfieldian argument about the restoration of meaning and experience through final participation. When Ransom, who is a self-conscious human and a Christian, is told that he needs to travel to Perelandra, he knows that it is for a purpose, to fight with "principalities and powers," but he also believes that it is not because he is "anyone in particular" (*P,* 24). He reaches Perelandra by means of a transporter resembling a "celestial coffin," which may signify Ransom's willingness to "die" to self and identify himself with Christ. When Weston arrives, Ransom recognizes the reason he has been sent: to protect the Green Lady; however, when deciding whether he will battle with the Un-man, he feels insufficient to the task. He has arguments with his "voluble self," which tells him that he is only a man, while the Un-man is a spirit. Ransom even argues with God for not sending a miracle, doubting the way God has chosen to do things on Perelandra and questioning his wisdom in sending Ransom to do the fighting. "Did Maledil *want* to lose worlds?" he asks (*P,* 142). Rather than experiencing communion with Maledil, Ransom has been ignoring his Presence, which never left him. As Ransom recognizes the Presence and eventually the Voice of God, he starts to learn more about himself. His self-consciousness becomes tied to his identity in God. He realizes that he himself was the miracle sent to Perelandra and recognizes that while he is limited if apart from God, "he did not know what he *could* do" (*P,* 141–42).

As the "Voice" of God drowns out the chatter of Ransom's "voluble self," it tells Ransom more about his purpose and the meaning of his life: "It is not for nothing that you are named Ransom" (*P,* 147), the Voice tells him. This assertion of Ransom's purpose revokes the earlier taunt of the Un-man, who had repeatedly called Ransom's name and greeted his response with the answer, "nothing," in a disheartening, demonic knock-knock joke. The Voice tells Ransom that even his name has a meaning: "A merely accidental resemblance of two sounds, was in truth no accident. The whole distinction between things accidental and things designed, like the distinction between fact and myth, was purely terrestrial." Ransom learns that before he had been born, before "Ransom" became his family name, "before *ransom* had been the name for a payment that delivers, . . . all these [meanings] had so stood together in eternity" as a fundamental unity (*P*, 148); Ransom's name is then a true metaphor. There is a preexisting relation between his name, his self-sacrifice to save the Green Lady from the Un-man, and the idea of a redeeming payment. However, it took communication with Maledil, the source of life, to discover this true meaning. Although through growing in his self-consciousness Ransom has learned the meaning of his own name, it is "in the name of the Father and of the Son and of the Holy Ghost" that Ransom finally fights the Un-man, for it is only in God that his name and mission have any meaning at all (*P*, 181).

Ransom's communion with Maledil increases as Ransom surrenders to his will. As he does so, he gains an assurance and trust. The day before the battle, "without any apparent movement of the will, as objective and unemotional as the reading on a dial, there [arose] before him, with perfect certitude, the knowledge 'about this time tomorrow you will have done the impossible'" (*P*, 149). Ransom takes this resoluteness into combat with the Un-man, waking on the morning of battle with "a full consciousness of his task" (*P*, 151). When he finally faces the monster, "Ransom found himself acting before he knew what he had done" (*P*, 152), punching, wrestling, chasing, and finally smashing in the head of the Un-man he was created to destroy.

As Ransom cooperates and participates in God's purpose, a gradual transformation takes place in his consciousness, and as it does, he affirms the Barfieldian idea that Reason splits and metaphor restores unified meaning. Traveling over the ocean on the back of a fish in pursuit of the Un-man, Ransom finds himself recognizing a *meaning* in Nature itself apart from man's endeavors: "The diffused meaning, the inscrutable character, which had been both in Tellus and Perelandra since they split off from the Sun, and which would be, in one sense, displaced by the advent of imperial man, yet in some other sense, not displaced at all, enfolded him on every side and caught him into itself" (*P*, 160).

Later in the pursuit, in the middle of a vast ocean, an exhausted Ransom becomes haunted by doubts about essential meaning. All the arguments he has heard denying unified meaning on Earth, especially arguments that "explain away" meaning using science, surface in his mind. Notice, in the following passage on what Ransom calls the "Empirical Bogey," the similarity to Barfield's theory of the loss of meaning through distinction and abstraction: "The Empirical Bogey, came surging into his mind—the great myth of our century with its gasses and galaxies, its light years and evolutions, its nightmare perspectives of simple arithmetic in which everything that can possibly hold significance for the mind becomes the mere by-product of essential disorder" (*P,* 164). Yet, even in the face of these doubts, Ransom affirms that the rational principle "begins to obscure perception of what is most worth remembering"[33] and that the power of metaphor, or "comparing" discovers meaning: "Part of him still knew that the size of a thing is its least important characteristic, *that the material universe derived from the comparing and mythopoeic power within him that very majesty* before which he was now asked to abase himself, and that mere numbers could not over-awe us unless we lent them, from our own resources, that awfulness which they themselves could no more supply than a banker's ledger [emphasis added]" (*P,* 164–65). Ransom understands that human rationality has separated the concrete and abstract meanings of words and objects and also realizes that "mythopoeic power" can re-infuse the concrete, measurable, material world with its original significance, in which material and immaterial, quantitative and qualitative values are reunited.

After victory against the Un-man, Ransom recovers and journeys to the top of a mountain, during which time he experiences profound contentment and reconnection with nature. As he recuperates from his battle, Ransom finds that he is now much like the Green Lady was when he first met her: "Neither the future nor the past really concerned him at this period. Wishing and fearing were modes of consciousness for which he seemed to have lost the faculty" (*P,* 187). This contentment continues as Ransom starts off on a journey, not knowing where he will end up, and when he reaches a mountain, we are told that "he had no desires and did not even think about reaching the top nor why he should reach it," yet he climbs up the mountain, content just to be climbing (*P,* 192). Ransom's perception is more immediate and concretely metaphorical. Like the Green Lady earlier in the book, Ransom is not concerned about time; he just keeps embracing and enjoying each scene he passes. When he encounters trees whose long, blue, streamerlike leaves rustle in the wind around him, he decides to call them "ripple trees," not whimsically, but simply and in truth, in much the same way the Green Lady named Ransom "Piebald" (*P,* 189).

It is after he reaches the top of the mountain that Ransom experiences what Barfield calls final participation. Because Ransom is self-conscious and lives after the rational age, he could never achieve original participation, nor would it be good if he could, for final participation is a *conscious*, understanding, and willing identification with the meaning of life. He can now consciously experience the unity of meaning. On the mountain, Ransom meets Malacandra, the masculine ruler of Mars, and Perelandra, the feminine ruler of Venus, and "what Ransom saw at that moment was the real meaning of gender" (*P*, 200). He immediately understands that linguistic assignments of gender in most of the world's languages are not projections of male or female characteristics on objects such as mountains or flowers but rather reflect a fundamental reality; therefore, recognition of the gender of an object is a true recognition of its unified meaning—yet another way language embodies meaning.

Finally, after Perelandra turns over authority on the planet to the King and Green Lady, Ransom participates in the "Great Dance" of celebration and praise to God. In the Great Dance, all participants are individually so unified with God, and through him, with each other, that Ransom "never knew which words were his or another's" (*P*, 204). This is also reminiscent of Barfield's definition of final participation as "man's Creator speaking with the voice and through the throat of a man."[34] Through a growth in self-consciousness, the self-consciousness that teaches Ransom about his identity in God, Ransom can now say "I am infinitely superfluous," while also understanding that he, like every other part of creation, is center of all (*P*, 217). As the chorus of "Blessed be He!" is repeated and the Great Dance proceeds, the movement "seemed to be woven out of the intertwining undulation of many cords or bands of light, leaping over and under one another and mutually embraced in arabesques and flower-like subtleties." It is the unity of *all* things, from "peoples, institutions, climates of opinion, civilizations, arts, sciences" to short-lived "flowers and insects" and even "universal truths or universal qualities" (*P*, 218–19). The Great Dance is the picture of the ultimate unity of all things of which Barfield speaks, but, more explicitly, it embodies the Christian truth: "All things are by Him and for Him. He utters Himself also for His own delight and sees that He is good. He is His own begotten and what proceeds from Him is Himself" (*P*, 217). Finally, when the dance is done, the animals have gone back to their everyday affairs, and Ransom must go back to Earth, the book ends with the words, "Then his consciousness was engulfed" (*P*, 222).

WESTON

Weston is the third character whose development of consciousness illuminates a Barfieldian sensibility. In *Out of the Silent Planet,* Weston
tries to construct a system of morality and duty based only on scientific
facts, justifying his conquest of other planets with the motivation of pre-
serving the human species. He has tried to answer the biggest questions
using only empirical evidence and premises, but by the time he arrives
in Perelandra, Weston has found, through the study of biology, that his
earlier impulse to preserve the species was irrational and unscientific; it
seems to him that he had mistakenly assumed the essential importance
of humans among the other species of the universe. Weston reaches the
conclusion, through studying emergent evolution, that "Man in himself
is nothing," a conclusion that Christians would agree with on its surface,
because, as Ransom finds, man is "superfluous." Yet, while Christians find
meaning in connection with God, the "source of Life," Weston now believes
that "the forward movement of Life—the growing spirituality—is everything" (*P,* 91). He tries to play off his "scientific spiritualism" as identical
to Christianity, co-opting Christian terminology for his "Life-force," but
Ransom immediately recognizes the difference and does not allow him
to be so loose with his meanings: "You see, I'm a Christian. And what we
mean by the Holy Ghost is *not* a blind, inarticulate purposiveness" (*P,* 91).
Weston's sloppy use of words and rejection of a true and definite meaning
suggest his rejection of true metaphors; he claims that his own vague,
transcendental beliefs may have been rendered inscrutable to Ransom by
the philologist's embrace of "early and revered associations," or ancient
unities, and that his religion of pure spirit is "in this new form the very
same truths" as Ransom's own Christian beliefs (*P,* 91).

However, the differences in the paths Weston and Ransom take to
find meaning and purpose become more obvious as Weston goes on to
say that the purpose for which he has been made, his goal, is "*pure* spirit:
the final vortex of self-thinking, self-originating activity" (*P,* 92), or, in
other words, pure abstraction. Weston himself not only suffers from his
own separation from meaning, but blasphemously seats the source of all
meaning in himself. Although he concedes that Man in itself is nothing,
Weston finds meaning in asserting his own independent will, rather than
finding meaning in self-sacrifice, surrender, and participation with God. In

Weston's morality and surrender to the life force, there is no hint of submission to a higher authority or law; he makes bold claims about his own
identity and authority, which reveal much about his self-consciousness:
"There is no possible distinction in concrete thought between me and the
universe. In so far as I am the conductor of the central forward pressure
of the universe, I am it. Do you see, you timid, scruple-mongering fool?
I *am* the Universe. I, Weston, am your God and your Devil" (*P,* 96).

At this moment, when Weston sounds most like the biblical angel
who asserts his independent will against God, Weston is transformed,
possessed by the Devil himself. Now the creature which Ransom names
the Un-man, or "something which was and was not Weston" (*P,* 107),
attempts to carry out the mission Weston described earlier, to spread
"self-thinking" to the inhabitants of Perelandra.

During his temptation of the Green Lady, the Un-Man's goal is to abstract
and alienate the woman's consciousness from her identity in unity with God.
He convinces her to look at herself, both figuratively and literally, by focusing on her identity as a woman, as beautiful, and as a willing being. "You
are becoming your own" (*P,* 115), he tells her, when she is becoming more
self-conscious. However, he does not want her merely to be self-conscious,
but self-willing and self-originating—not simply to walk alongside God, but
to live irrespective of him. He wants her to disobey Maledil's command
against sleeping on the Fixed Land, and even tells the Green Lady that
Maledil would want her to disobey, that he would take pleasure in his creation becoming more independent. The Un-man's strategy includes telling
her tragic stories of women on Earth and showing her to herself in a mirror:
"The image of her beautiful body had been offered to her only as a means
to awake the far more perilous image of her great soul. The external, as it
were, dramatic conception of the self was the enemy's true aim" (*P,* 138–39).

Other characteristics mark the abstraction of the Un-man from the world.
For example, he purposelessly destroys and dominates nature rather than
participating with it, and he is responsible for the first death on Perelandra.
Ransom wakes one morning and finds a hideously damaged animal, a frog
with a great, V-shaped gash in its back. He is devastated by this one spoiled
animal, but then sees a whole trail of similarly mutilated frogs leading to
Weston, who is throwing another "bleeding ruin" away from him in sense-
less, intentional waste (*P,* 110). Weston also shows cruelty to the fish he
rides when running away from Ransom (*P,* 158). Such malice is a reflection

of Weston's disgust for the physical world, which, not being "pure spirit," is contemptible to him. On this point, Lewis evokes the attitude of Milton's Satan, who has a deep disgust for the physical and extreme contempt for the necessity of taking on flesh to tempt Eve.

Lewis gives a well-developed description of how Weston, as he is separated from the world around him, is also separated from himself. Ransom watches as Weston's consciousness disintegrates, divides, and destroys itself. He observes of the Un-man, "Ages ago [he] had been a Person: but the ruins of personality now survived in it only as weapons at the disposal of a furious self-exiled negation" (*P*, 156). As he chases down the Un-man, Ransom feels pity, since the "remnants of Weston's consciousness" might possibly remain imprisoned in his body (*P*, 157). Lewis stylistically represents this breakdown in a stream of consciousness passage when the Un-man momentarily lets Weston control his body, which still seems out of control: "That boy keeps on shutting the windows. That's all right, they've taken off my head and put someone else's on me. I'll soon be all right now. They won't let me see my press cuttings. So then I went and told him that if they didn't want me in the first Fifteen they could jolly well do without me, see" (*P*, 129).

What Weston says to Ransom is nonsense. The words reflect Weston's broken consciousness, which is being ripped apart by its possessor, the way he ripped apart the frogs. It is as if Weston's memories and thoughts are being emulsified in a blender; in the end, after Weston is destroyed, Ransom remarks that he is "one whom Satan has digested" (*P*, 73). It appears that this destruction illustrates the more complete disintegration of Weston's imagination. According to Wolfe's "Essential Speech," the Un-Man represents the total corruption of the imagination, the faculty involved in rediscovering true associations between concrete and abstract meaning, and as a result, his speech is at times garbled and meaningless, having no referential value.[35] Separated from concrete reality, abstractions are meaningless. Weston despises the concrete and the physical part of human nature, while humans are by nature unified beings, both physical and spiritual, and not just the combination of the two but something other. It is as if Weston, in his attempt to divorce the spiritual from physical, thereby destroying his humanity, embodies the process of abstraction Barfield attributes to the Rational principle. As a result of this split, Weston's humanity itself is eaten away, and he himself becomes meaningless (*P*, 130).

Meaning is a preoccupation for all three characters, but it is only Weston who ultimately denies the existence of meaning at all. Weston's first words on Perelandra are, "May I ask you, Dr. Ransom, what is the meaning of this?" (*P,* 119). This common question is easy to pass over, yet it is an early indication of the central struggle for Weston, and for all of the characters: "What or where is the meaning?" Weston, first, seems to believe that he has found true Meaning. He has discarded his earlier goal of utility to the human race and rejected what he calls the "outworn theological technicalities" of religion, penetrating "the crust" and finding that "the Meaning beneath it is as true and as living as ever" (*P,* 91). He associates this meaning with "spirituality" and the mind, and he mistakenly believes that Christians worship God because he is pure spirit (*P,* 93). Even at the outset, however, Weston is undermining meaning itself, using words loosely and denying any absolute meaning outside of himself. Later, when tempting the Green Lady, he perverts the meanings of words like *courage* and *duty,* and at other times lies outright, telling the Green Lady, for example, that God desires her disobedience. During this whole time, however, Ransom is aware that Weston's consciousness is imprisoned and being destroyed by Satan, who chants the word "nothing" at him, trying to cause Ransom to doubt his own meaning and purpose. The Un-man makes a formidable enemy, particularly because there is no possible communication with it: "What could you say—what appeal or threat could have any meaning—to *that?*" Ransom asks (*P,* 110). While his consciousness is digested, Weston has a few somewhat lucid moments, in which he finally denies all meaning: he has now seen through the crust and there is absolutely nothing there. Even Weston's gestures are now "meaningless" (*P,* 166). Past the rind of the forbidden fruit, Weston finds that "all the colours and pleasant shapes are merely where it ends, where it ceases to be. Inside, what do you get? Darkness, worms, heat, pressure, salt, suffocation, stink" (*P,* 169). Ransom and the Green Lady, however, find meaning. They recognize that "there is no way out of the centre save into the Bent Will which casts itself into the Nowhere" (*P,* 216), which is exactly what Weston has done. On a memorial to Weston, Ransom carved that he "submitted his will to the bent eldil" (*P,* 188). Weston finds that nothing is beyond the crust and ends up nihilistically and demonically embracing that Nothing in his rejection of meaning.

The way in which C. S. Lewis develops the consciousness of each of the three characters—the Green Lady, Ransom, and Weston—corresponds strikingly to Barfield's theory of the development of language and meaning, and of its implications for language. The Green Lady initially does not even recognize her identity as separate from God, as in original participation. She has such close communion with him that the ancient language she speaks with Ransom and Weston is almost unnecessary. As she grows in her self-consciousness and, as a result, obeys God more fully, however, she experiences complete communion or final participation. Ransom's consciousness is in a different position from hers because of his citizenship of Earth, which has fallen. Because of the Fall, language and concepts on Earth are abstracted and bent, tending toward meaninglessness. Through obedience to God's will, Ransom experiences communion with God or final participation, learning the unified meaning of everything that takes part in the Great Dance. Weston, in rejecting God and his truth, seeks to find meaning through asserting his own will; as a result, no remnant of communion exists in him, either with creation or the Creator.

In *Perelandra*, we see how C. S. Lewis gently corrects and brings to life his friend's influential theory of language, consciousness, and meaning. Whatever debt readers around the world may have to C. S. Lewis, there can be no doubt that he himself was indebted to his friend and "unofficial" teacher, Owen Barfield.

Notes

1. Colin Duriez and David Porter, *The Inklings Handbook* (St. Louis, Mo.: Chalice Press, 2001), 68.

2. Lionel Adey, *C. S. Lewis's "Great War" with Owen Barfield* (Victoria, B.C.: English Literary Studies, 1978), 22.

3. Owen Barfield, *Poetic Diction* (Middletown, Conn.: Wesleyan Univ. Press, 1973), 55–56.

4. Owen Barfield, *Saving The Appearances* (Middletown, Conn.: Wesleyan Univ. Press, 1988), 116.

5. Owen Barfield, *Poetic Diction*, 64.

6. Ibid., 62–63.

7. Quoted in Adey, *Lewis's "Great War,"* 20.

8. Barfield, *Poetic Diction*, 80, 74, 92.

9. Barfield, *Saving the Appearances*, 122.

10. Owen Barfield, *Speaker's Meaning* (Middletown, Conn.: Wesleyan Univ. Press, 1967), 56–57.

11. Ibid., 57.

12. *Owen Barfield: Man and Meaning,* video, directed by Ben Levin, produced by G. B. Tennyson and David Lavery (Encino, Calif.: OwenArts, 1996).

13. Barfield, *Saving the Appearances,* 41.

14. Barfield, *Poetic Diction,* 86.

15. Adey, *Lewis's "Great War,"* 21.

16. Barfield, *Poetic Diction,* 32–33, 63, 143, 85–86, 118, 43.

17. Adey, *Lewis's "Great War,"* 89.

18. Barfield, *Poetic Diction,* 86, 88.

19. Adey, *Lewis's "Great War,"* 37, 109, 29.

20. Barfield, *Saving the Appearances,* 169, 170.

21. *Owen Barfield: Man and Meaning.*

22. Rom. 11:36 (English Standard Version).

23. Edwin Woodruff Tait, "Owen Barfield: Un-Regressed Pilgrim" (Paper presented at the Seventh Frances White Colloquium on C. S. Lewis and Friends, Taylor University, Upland, Ind., 2010,) *Inklings Forever* 7 (2010), http://library.taylor.edu/dotAsset/9d2a300b-4599–458b-a9a8–8c19b3286c26.pdf, accessed July 31, 2011.

24. C. S. Lewis, "The 'Great War' Letters," in Lewis, *CL* III, ed. Walter Hooper (New York: HarperCollins, 2007), 1599.

25. Gregory Wolfe, "Essential Speech: Language and Meaning in the Ransom Trilogy," in *Word and Story in C. S. Lewis,* ed. Peter J. Schakel and Charles A. Huttar (Columbia, Mo.: Univ. of Missouri Press, 1991), 58.

26. Ibid., 57, 61, 80.

27. Ibid., 75, 78, 105, 69.

28. Ibid., 68, 60, 68.

29. Ibid., 69, 70, 60.

30. Barfield, *Saving the Appearances,* 169.

31. C. S. Lewis, *P* (New York: Macmillan, 1944), 114.

32. Barfield, *Saving the Appearances,* 171–72.

33. Barfield, *Poetic Diction,* 106.

34. Barfield, *Saving the Appearances,* 170.

35. Wolfe, "Essential Speech."

Myth, Pluralism, and Choice

Perelandra *and Lewis on Religious Truth*

MERIEL PATRICK

In his essay "Myth Became Fact," Lewis argues that there is a dichotomy between human thought and human experience: intellectually, we can grasp only the abstract, but we can experience only the concrete. If we attempt to examine the objects of our experience, we cease to experience them as themselves: they instantly become mere instances or examples of a particular abstract concept. "The more lucidly we think," Lewis argues, "the more we are cut off: the more deeply we enter into reality, the less we can think. You cannot *study* Pleasure in the moment of the nuptial embrace, nor repentance while repenting, nor analyse the nature of humour while roaring with laughter. But when else can you really know these things?"[1]

Myths, Lewis suggests, offer us a partial solution: "In the enjoyment of a great myth we come nearest to experiencing as a concrete what can otherwise be understood only as an abstraction."[2] It is not simply that the elements of the myth represent abstract truths: if that were the case, says Lewis, it would be a mere allegory. Instead, the myth allows us to experience (or as Lewis puts it, to taste) rather than simply to have intellectual knowledge—but the thing that we are tasting turns out to be a universal principle.

Lewis does not offer a definition of *myth* in this essay, but it seems plain that he understands a myth to be a story that embodies such universal principles: he describes myth as "the father of innumerable truths."[3] He goes on to argue in the rest of the essay that Christianity is a myth that is also a fact. The story alone is one from which one can derive spiritual sustenance (regardless, Lewis thinks, of whether one believes it or not), but it also happens to describe events that really occurred.

It seems clear that, in the history of Perelandra, the story of Ransom, Weston, and the Lady would fall into the same category of factual myth. Indeed, as he wrestles with the prospect of attempting to slay the Evil One and ponders the mythological character of what is apparently being asked of him, Ransom perceives that the very distinction between myth and fact will have no meaning on Perelandra: it is a purely terrestrial one. It is, he comes to see, "part and parcel of the unhappy division between soul and body which resulted from the Fall."[4]

Taken in the context of Lewis's argument in "Myth Became Fact," this presumably means that Lewis sees the Perelandrans as beings who retain intact the ability to have that experience of universal principles for which fallen humans must now turn to myths. It seems that soul or mind is what does the abstract thinking, and that body is what experiences—although (as presumably neither Lewis nor Ransom would wish to claim that all experience is purely physical in nature) perhaps we should see *body* as being used in a partially figurative sense here. In the human story, the body itself becomes an object of shame—hence Adam's and Eve's post-Fall desire to hide their nakedness—and healing of the rift between body and soul begins with the Incarnation, when God, who is pure spirit, unites himself with a human body.

In his apologetic work *The Problem of Pain* (published in 1940, three years before *Perelandra* appeared), Lewis devotes a chapter to the Fall of humanity. He spends some time speculating about the possible experience of Paradisal man,[5] and he puts forward several ideas that resurface in his depiction of the Lady in *Perelandra*. Of particular relevance is his suggestion that unfallen man was fully conscious of and exercised complete control over the workings of his body: "His organic processes obeyed the law of his own will, not the law of nature. His organs sent up appetites to the judgement seat of will not because they had to, but because he chose. Sleep meant to him not the stupor which we undergo, but willed and conscious repose—he remained awake to enjoy the pleasure and duty of sleep" (*PP,* 65–66). Compare this to Ransom's impressions when he sees the Lady sleeping: "Her face was full of expression and intelligence, and the limbs looked as if they were ready at any moment to leap up, and altogether she gave the impression that sleep was not a thing that happened to her but an action which she performed" (*P,* 256).

This control over the body, Lewis argues, was a delegation of divine authority: God ruled unfallen human bodies through unfallen human spirits. When the human spirit rebelled against him, however, this was no longer possible, and instead God began to rule the body "in a more external way, not by the laws of spirit, but by those of nature" (*PP,* 70). The consequences were ruinous. Not only were human beings now subject to physical infirmity and death, but "desires began to come up into the mind of man, not as his reason chose, but just as the biochemical and environmental facts happened to cause them. And the mind itself fell under the psychological laws of association and the like which God had made to rule the psychology of the higher anthropoids. . . . Thus human spirit from being the master of human nature became a mere lodger in its own house, or even a prisoner" (*PP,* 70–71). This deterioration is accompanied by a corruption of the spirit itself: it turns away from God and becomes focused on itself.

The consequences of this change in the human condition include one of which most of us are all too aware: consistently making the right choices becomes much harder. Because the desires of the flesh are no longer one with those of the spirit, we experience internal conflict, and we are often driven by (or are slaves to) our appetites. The state we find ourselves in contrasts sharply with that of the Lady, who feels no impulse toward gluttony or unchastity and has no interest in possessions.

This idea manifests itself in one of the central themes of *Perelandra:* that of making the choice between embracing the good that God sends us—or, to use the Lady's image, plunging into the wave that Maleldil rolls toward us—and turning aside from it to something of our own choosing. Although we—or at any rate our fleshly appetites—regard whatever it is that we are tempted to turn toward as something good, it will inevitably cease to be so if we must step out of God's omnibenevolent will to gain it. The central issue seems to be one of control: whether we are willing to put ourselves entirely in the hands of the one who made us, or whether we are determined to be masters of our own destiny, whatever the cost may be. In the final scenes of the novel, the Lady realizes that this was the essence of the temptation she faced, although it manifested itself in the form of the prospect of dwelling on the Fixed Land. "Why should I desire the Fixed," she asks, "except to make sure—to be able on one day to command where I should be the next and what should happen to me? It was to reject the wave—to draw my hands out of Maleldil's, to say to Him, 'Not thus, but thus'—to put in our own power what times should roll towards us" (*P*, 335).

We may also note that Ransom identifies a similar temptation in himself before he even meets the Lady. His first taste of Perelandran food is the yellow gourds, and after the intense pleasure of the first one, he has to resist an impulse to pick a second, despite the fact that he is no longer hungry or thirsty. A little later he recognizes that what lies behind this impulse is a common human experience: the "itch to have things over again, as if life were a film that could be unrolled twice or even made to work backwards" (*P*, 186)—that is, a desire to exercise control over what comes next or how many times an experience is repeated. Ransom wonders whether this may in fact be the root of all evil—and whether money, which has been called that, only exercises such a fatal fascination for many of our race because it provides the means of controlling what happens to us—it is "a defense against chance" and "a means of arresting the unrolling of the film" (*P*, 186).

Digging a little deeper, we can see that there seem to be two competing concepts of freedom here. There is a sense in which opting to control one's own destiny gives one a much wider range of choices. Instead of simply waiting for and then embracing whatever good things God chooses to send us, we can go in search of whichever good happens to appeal to us most at the time. With a little advance planning, we may not even need to go in search of it: we can arrange to have our chosen pleasures easily available to us whenever we want them. Moreover, it is not just the number of choices, but the significance of them that seems much greater. The Perelandrans do have a range of options open to them: they might decide to go swimming one day, island-hopping the next, and to visit the Fixed Land (although not, of course, to stay there) on a third. But human beings can make choices that will have a much larger impact on their own lives and those of other people: for example, they can choose to work hard, or to be lazy, to become a doctor and save lives, or to become a terrorist and bring about death and carnage. Moreover, some of those choices will beget other choices: for example, choosing to work hard may result in having plenty of money to spend as one wishes. Things won't necessarily always go smoothly—in the current economic climate, many people are all too aware that hard work is no guarantee of financial security—but even bad fortune brings further choices: to bear it with fortitude, to fight harder for what one wants, or to give up and despair.

However, despite our much wider range of options, it is not at all clear that the Perelandrans are less free than we are. Very often the choices we face arise from the conflicts we find within ourselves, which Lewis would attribute to the division between body and soul that resulted from the Fall. Our flesh wants one thing, our minds or souls want another. We may be aware that a certain action is very much less than the best one available to us—aware, even, that we will regret it as soon as it is done—and yet still feel a powerful compulsion to perform it.[6] Someone may know that scratching a rash will only make it worse, or be perfectly certain that committing adultery will cause heartbreak to everyone involved, and yet still choose that course of action. We may firmly resolve to live our lives in the way that we believe to be the best, and we will still be tempted away from that resolution by factors that we know to be irrational. More than that, there may be difficulties in even making such a resolution, as we frequently find ourselves genuinely uncertain about what the best course of action is. In the words of Jean-Paul Sartre, we are condemned to be free,[7] and that very freedom often seems to result in behavior which from a rational perspective we consider undesirable.

By comparison, the Perelandrans lead an untroubled existence—at least prior to Weston's arrival on the planet. It is not in fact the case that they have no choices to make, or only trivial ones; on the contrary, they are continually choosing to embrace whatever good Maleldil sends them. But the choice is so natural that until it is brought to her attention by Ransom, the Lady does not even notice that this is what is happening. "'I thought,' she said, 'that I was carried in the will of Him I love, but now I see that I walk with it. I thought that the good things He sent me drew me into them as the waves lift the islands; but now I see that it is I who plunge into them with my own arms and legs, as when we go swimming. . . . I thought we went along paths—but it seems there are no paths. The going itself is the path'" (*P,* 205–6).

We might say that while the Lady has fewer options than fallen humanity, she has far more freedom. Alternatively, we could borrow from the language of political philosophy and distinguish between negative and positive freedom. Negative freedom is simply freedom from external restrictions. Positive freedom, however, implies freedom from internal constraints—that is, the things that keep us from acting as we wish—or the freedom to behave as a rational person would choose. Human beings, perhaps, have more negative freedom, but the Lady far excels us in her level of positive freedom. (It is interesting to notice that Lewis uses almost Sartresque language when describing the Tempter's response to the Lady's doubts about acting without consulting her husband: he tells her that "The King must be forced to be free" [*P*, 262]. We can surmise that the "freedom" that would result if she yields to the Tempter would be of the same type experienced by fallen humanity—the type, that is, which Sartre bemoans—although, as *Perelandra* and *Being and Nothingness* were first published in the same year, the echo is presumably not deliberate.)

There is a further aspect of the difference between the Lady's condition and ours that brings us back to the distinction—or lack of it—between myth and fact. A large part of the reason that the Lady finds it easy to embrace what Maleldil sends her is the intimacy of her relationship with him. She has not the slightest doubt about his existence or trustworthiness, and on many subjects she hears him speak to her clearly. She has no serious choices to make regarding religious belief: Maleldil is as real to her as the physical world around her—or perhaps more real—and his presence is as easily perceived. For human beings, however, the situation is very different. In our fallen world, certainty about God is not always easy to acquire—and even if we are personally sure of what we believe, we are likely to find our views disputed by others with different perspectives. The splintering of truth into fact and myth results in a bewildering array of options. We find ourselves faced with a multitude of religious narratives, all of which claim to reveal eternal truths.

Modern, pluralist approaches to religion are inclined to treat these as equally valuable. The existence of some form of transcendent or ultimate reality is acknowledged—what John Hick calls the Real, and others have called the Numinous—but its precise nature is taken to be beyond human comprehension. Hence, different religious traditions are held to reflect different aspects of it, or different ways of experiencing it.[8] No tradition has a monopoly on religious truth. Pluralism endorses the freedom of the individual to select what he or she personally finds helpful or attractive. The variety of religious traditions is not infrequently viewed as a positive thing: it extends our power to choose—to determine our own destiny—beyond merely temporal matters, to include the nature of the eternal verities we elect to accept.

Shortly after he arrives on Perelandra, Weston puts forward a view of the world that may be seen as a somewhat extreme variety of pluralism. He informs Ransom that his ideas have undergone a radical change since they last met: his mission is now to promote "the forward movements of Life" and "to spread spirituality" (*P*, 225). This means, he claims, that nothing now divides him and Ransom "except a few outworn theological technicalities with which organised religion has unhappily allowed itself to get incrusted" (*P*, 225). When Ransom protests that the Holy Spirit of the Christian tradition does not in fact bear any real resemblance to the "blind, inarticulate purposiveness" of which Weston speaks, Weston assures him: "'Early and revered associations may have put it out of your power to recognise in this new form the very same truths which religion has so long preserved and which science is now at last re-discovering. But whether you can see it or not, believe me, we are talking about exactly the same thing'" (*P*, 225). But Weston goes much further than this. When Ransom suggests that the fact that something is a spirit does not imply that it must be good, remarking that after all, "the Devil is a spirit" (*P*, 227), Weston replies that the widespread religious tendency to "breed pairs of opposites" (*P*, 227)—to conceive of the world in terms of contrasting realities such as God and the Devil, or heaven and hell—is a direct result of the Life-Force implanting portraits of itself in human minds. In other words, there is a single Spirit or Life-Force, and the Christian God and the Devil are both pictures of it. While the two may emphasize different features, they reflect the same underlying reality.

An example of a slightly different sort occurs in *The Great Divorce*, where Lewis depicts a liberal theologian who, even on the outskirts of heaven, refuses to commit himself to—or even acknowledge the existence of—a single definite truth about religion. He is adamant that no one will be penalized for what he calls "honest opinions," and in that sense he seems to fall into the category of those who hold that it doesn't particularly matter what one believes, as long as one does so sincerely. But in his case the rot has gone further: he has devoted his life to the intellectual investigation of religion but in the process has lost his taste for answers, and instead he has come to regard the questioning as the purpose of the whole process. When he is offered definitive answers, and with them the opportunity to see the face of God, he recoils, and insists that he must have "an atmosphere of inquiry" and "free play of the Mind."[9] His is not a pluralism in which many surface "truths" may all reflect something of the deeper reality, but one where the surface has become all that matters. The tragic irony is that although embracing their own particular versions of spirituality may have begun as an exercise of freedom, it ultimately becomes a trap from which neither can escape.

Lewis himself was no pluralist. While he did hold that nonfactual myths could be vehicles of truth, and that many pre-Christian traditions include elements that prefigure the Christian story, this is quite different from suggesting that all these traditions have an equal claim to being regarded as truth. They don't: they're true to precisely the extent that they reflect the myth that is also a fact—Christianity—and no more. The only safe (and the only intellectually respectable) course of action is to sift through the variety of traditions on offer to locate the truth. This is not a matter of choice, but rather of discovery and then submission. Indeed, we might say that the myth that is also a fact is the ultimate God-sent good that must be embraced: the wave we must plunge into.

In his introduction to *The Great Divorce*, Lewis writes about the distinction between good and evil, and I do not think it is too much of a stretch to take what he says to also apply to religious truth: "We are not living in a world where all roads are radii of a circle and where all, if followed long enough, will therefore draw gradually nearer and finally meet at the centre: rather in a world where every road, after a few miles, forks into two, and each of those into two again, and at each fork you must make a decision. . . . I do not think that all who choose wrong roads perish; but their rescue consists in being put back on the right road" (*TGD*, 7).

However, something of a paradox remains. It is easy for the Lady to plunge into whatever waves Maleldil sends her because of her clear knowledge of the unfractured truth, and because of the unity of body and soul that means she is not subject to the irrational impulses that beset fallen creatures. And it seems undeniable that it is good for her to be in this state. But at the same time, this ease means she lacks an opportunity that humans have in abundance: that of moving toward maturity through making a more challenging choice—one where the right course is not so obvious and requires her to exercise her own judgment. This is only made possible through the advent of the Tempter in Weston's body—and by a further factor: a temporary cessation of, or at least a reduction in, the clear communication with God to which she is accustomed. When the Tempter first begins to encourage the Lady to think of living on the Fixed Land and suggests that she may learn wisdom from him as well as from Maleldil and her husband, she comments that Maleldil is not putting much into her mind about the questions he raises (*P,* 238). This is apparently an unusual experience for her; Maleldil has previously given her answers when she needed them.[10] It seems that the divine voice is being deliberately withheld.

So while in many ways her freedom is much greater than that of fallen creatures, it appears that if she is to have the full range of choices necessary to allow her to grow into the creature God intends her to be, an element resembling one of the results of the Fall must be introduced: her certainty has to be shaken. The Lady thus finds herself facing competing accounts of Maleldil's prohibition of living on the Fixed Land, and she must reason her way through these to a decision.

But this is not the whole story: it is unclear that a mere mistake in reasoning would count as a true sin. The Tempter's aim is not simply to persuade her to take the action but to do so in a way that will make her the heroine of the piece—in short, to put herself, rather than Maleldil, at the center. In *The Problem of Pain,* Lewis suggests that such an act (which he describes as one of self-will or self-idolatry) is "the only sin that can be conceived as the Fall" (*PP,* 68), because it is the only imaginable sin that is both sufficiently heinous and possible for one not subject to the temptations faced by fallen humanity.

In order to be truly tempted in this respect, the Lady must first come to see herself as a being capable of such a declaration of independence: an entity able to choose in whose hands she will place (or attempt to place) her destiny. We have already seen that when Ransom first meets her, she barely even realizes that she is choosing to embrace Maleldil's will; at the point when this becomes clear to her, she wonders at the fact that Maleldil has made her "so separate from Himself," and exclaims, "It is delight with terror in it!" (*P,* 205). Her awareness of her separateness grows as the book progresses, and while this brings danger, it also brings opportunity. In the midst of her period of temptation, Ransom muses on the choice she faces: "Certainly it must be part of the Divine plan that this happy creature should mature, should become more and more a creature of free choice, should become, in a sense, more distinct from God and from her husband in order thereby to be at one with them in a richer fashion. . . . This present temptation, if conquered, would itself be the next, and greatest, step in the same direction: an obedience freer, more reasoned, more conscious than any she had known before, was being put in her power" (*P*, 264–65).

The Lady does resist the temptation, and the obedience Ransom talks of results in the freedom of Perelandra's inhabitants being not only protected but extended. Moreover, the experience ultimately brings knowledge: by the end of the book, the Perelandrans have a true understanding of the nature of good and evil. The King tells Ransom: "'There is an ignorance of evil that comes from being young: there is a darker ignorance that comes from doing it, as men by sleeping lose the knowledge of sleep. . . . Maleldil has brought us out of the one ignorance, and we have not entered the other. It was by the Evil One himself that he brought us out of the first. Little did that dark mind know the errand on which he really came to Perelandra!" (*P*, 335).

Both body and soul and myth and fact remain united on Perelandra. More than this, they become so closely bound together that it seems impossible that their unity should ever be threatened again. But the method by which this is achieved is one that we may find surprising. The deepest obedience is gained only by learning what it would mean to live for oneself rather than for God—and perhaps even by seeing some glimmer of the appeal of this. The deepest knowledge is reached by the shaking of certainty. Paradoxically, it seems that full unity can be brought about only by the advent of at least the shadow of a fissure.

NOTES

1. C. S. Lewis, "Myth Became Fact," in Lewis, *EC* II (London: HarperCollins, 2000), 138–42; quotation on p. 140, emphasis in original.

2. Ibid.

3. Ibid., 141.

4. C. S. Lewis, *P* (London: Pan, 1989), 274.

5. C. S. Lewis, *PP* (London: Fontana, 1957), 65–67.

6. The classic biblical statement of this internal conflict is, of course, Paul's: "I do not understand my own actions. . . . For I do not do the good I want, but the evil I do not want is what I keep on doing" (Rom. 7:15–19 [English Standard Version]).

7. See, for example, Sartre's *Being and Nothingness: An Essay on Phenomeno-logical Ontology*, trans. Hazel E. Barnes (London: Routledge, 2003), 462: "I am condemned to be free. This means that no limits to my freedom can be found except freedom itself or, if you prefer, that we are not free to cease being free."

8. See, for example, Hick's essay "On Conflicting Religious Truth Claims," *Religious Studies* 19, no. 4 (1983): 487: "The great world faiths embody different perceptions and conceptions of, and correspondingly different responses to, the Real or the Ultimate from within the different cultural ways of being human."

9. C. S. Lewis, *TGD* (London: Fontana, 1972), 37, 40, 41.

10. When Ransom tells her that living on the fixed land is not forbidden in his world, for example, Maleldil confirms this (*P,* 210), and when she wishes to try scraping the skin off her knee to experience pain, Maleldil tells her not to (*P,* 214–15).

Frightful Freedom

Perelandra *as Imaginative Theodicy*

BRUCE R. JOHNSON

In a letter to his old friend Arthur Greeves, dated September 12, 1933, C. S. Lewis responds to a question Arthur had raised about "God and evil."[1] The classic academic dilemma, as Lewis would later summarize it in *The Problem of Pain*, goes like this: "If God were good, He would wish to make His creatures perfectly happy, and if God were almighty He would be able to do what he wished. But the creatures are not happy. Therefore God lacks either goodness, or power, or both."[2] Yet this was not precisely Arthur's question. Instead, as Lewis put it, Arthur was focused on "a more personal, practical, and intimate problem" (*CL* II, 121), namely, whether God sympathizes with the evil inside us, with our evil will. Lewis does a fair job of responding to this, focusing much of his attention on human temptation. But it is not quite enough. In the end, Lewis concludes, "I expect I have said all these things before: if so, I hope they have not wasted a letter. Alas! They are so (comparatively) easy to say: so hard, so *all but* impossible to go on *feeling* when the strain comes" (*CL* II, 125).

Lewis offers a similar caveat in his 1940 preface to *The Problem of Pain*. There he quotes from Walter Hilton's work, *Scale of Perfection:* "I feel myself so far from true feeling of that I speak, that I can naught else but cry mercy and desire after it as I may" (*PP*, vii). Lewis adds, "the only purpose of the book [*The Problem of Pain*] is to solve the intellectual problem raised by suffering; for the far higher task of teaching fortitude and patience I was never fool enough to suppose myself qualified, nor have I anything to offer my readers except my conviction that when pain is to be borne, a little courage helps more than much knowledge, a little human sympathy more than much courage, and the least tincture of the love of God more than all" (*PP,* vii–viii).

Those three small pieces of advice are actually quite helpful—so much so that Lewis will find a way of dispensing them again in 1941, as he begins to write *Perelandra.* They are important because there is so much more at stake here than simply an intellectual argument. People suffer. They experience pain. As they do, it is often hard for Christians to hold on to hope in the face of the "more personal, practical, and intimate" problems of evil. Doing so generally takes moving beyond the exclusive arena of rational arguments to the additional arenas of the will, emotions, and mystical experience. Resolving the tensions between faith and painful reality takes courage (what could be called the volitional resolution), or sympathy for the plight of others (the emotional resolution), or the love of God (the mystical resolution). Examples of such responses to pain are numerous and diverse: from the joyful spirituals sung by African American slaves to the mystical poetry written in prison by St. John of the Cross. Each attempts to build a bridge across the intellectual gap where rational explanations for evil become insufficient. Such efforts are not strictly "theodicy" because they move beyond the boundaries of pure intellectual reasoning. Yet they are something. When such movement occurs within a work of fiction, it could be termed *imaginative theodicy.*

Because C. S. Lewis was a master at several different genres of literature, he was able to explore these three themes imaginatively as he shifted from his self-described "amateur theology" to the space "thriller" *Perelandra.* In that novel, the character of Elwin Ransom grows spiritually as sympathy, courage, and the love of God are stirred up in him. Other theological themes are also present, to be sure. But this is one of the key "takeaways," one of the practical bits of theological advice, that Lewis was hoping to smuggle past the watchful dragons of modern culture into the lives of his readers. Putting these lessons into a novel has the added advantage of allowing readers to experience vicariously the weight of these three resolutions as they identify with the hero, Ransom, as he works through them. In *The Problem of Pain,* Lewis states that he is "aiming at an intellectual, not an emotional effect" (*PP,* 55). In *Perelandra,* because the genre is different, he is less constrained. Instead of "telling us a thing was terrible," he can "describe it so that we'll be terrified."[3] So, for instance, as Ransom realizes how much is a stake in the "frightful freedom" of his own free decision,[4] the reader agonizes along with the hero as he works through that volitional resolution.

In order to examine how Lewis presents this imaginative theodicy, it will first be necessary to cite in *Perelandra* echoes of some of the classical arguments of theodicy. Next, I will explore the spiritual growth of the main character, as he attains emotional, volitional, and mystical resolutions. Finally I will comment on why Lewis moved from the 1940 academic approach of *The Problem of Pain* to the 1943 imaginative theodicy of *Perelandra.*

Where in *Perelandra* do we find echoes of the classic arguments of theodicy? These traditional efforts to reconcile God's goodness and power with painful reality address, among other forms of suffering, evil that stems from human choices (such as a drunk driver who injures a pedestrian), pain that serves a greater good (like the pain a dentist provides), and suffering that refines the soul (such as sitting through a boring but enlightening lecture). In *Perelandra,* such arguments find expression in the series of dialogues between Ransom, Tinidril, and the Un-man. For instance, there is the argument concerning free will, a recurring theme for Lewis. In *Mere Christianity,* Lewis explains that "God created things which had free will. That means creatures which can go either wrong or right. . . . Of course God knew what would happen if they used their freedom the wrong way; apparently He thought it worth the risk."[5] In *The Problem of Pain,* Lewis states the obvious: "We have used our free will to become very bad" (*PP,* 43). Could a different choice be made on a different world? In *Perelandra,* Ransom asks the Green Lady, "Where can you taste the joy of obeying unless He bids you do something for which His bidding is the *only* reason?" Tinidril responds, "Oh, how well I see it! We cannot walk out of Maleldil's will: but he has given us a way out of *our* will" (*P,* 118).

This brings up a corollary to the free will argument: freedom is necessary if people are to truly love their Maker. Love that is demanded or forced is not real love. In other words, "their freedom," says Lewis, "is simply that of making a single naked choice—of loving God more than the self or the self more than God" (*PP,* 18). This is why God takes the risk. Ransom hopes the Green Lady will quickly make the right choice, ending all the drama on Perelandra. Early on, this seems possible. Trinidril's first encounter with evil, in the form of the Un-man, ends with her praising Christ: "How beautiful is Maledil [i.e., Christ] and how wonderful are all his works: perhaps He will bring out of me daughters as much greater than I as I am greater than the beasts. It will be better than I thought" (*P*, 118). Ransom is relieved, and falls asleep that night with "the feeling of a great disaster averted" (*P*, 107).

However, neither the drama nor the temptation will end that quickly. This gives some time for a few more echoes of classic arguments of theodicy. Not much more can be said through the voice of Trinidril, since she is an unfallen creature. But there are other characters in this cast—Weston, for instance. One avenue of theodicy contends that some evil is so deep, or on so massive a scale (for example, the Holocaust, 9/11, or the genocide in Rwanda), that human free will is an inadequate explanation for it. In such cases, some Christians have discerned demonic power at work. Ransom begins to understand that this is what is happening in the Un-man: "Weston's body, traveling in a space-ship, had been the bridge by which something else had invaded Perelandra—whether that supreme and original evil whom in Mars they call The Bent One, or one of his lesser followers, made no difference. Ransom was all gooseflesh, and his knees kept getting in each other's way" (*P*, 111–12).

In his 1941 essay "Evil and God," Lewis explains, "There was never any question of tracing *all* evil to man; in fact, the New Testament has a good deal more to say about dark superhuman powers than about the fall of Adam."[6] It also can be noted that the Un-man diabolically twists around the "greater good" argument of theodicy. If the sin on one planet led to the Incarnation, let sin enter another planet so that Christ may be incarnate again (and presumably die again).

This is the point in the story at which the hero, Elwin Ransom, demonstrates "the old Christian doctrine of being made 'perfect through suffering'" (*PP*, 93). He struggles within himself, thinking, "Unfair . . . unfair. How could Maleldil expect him to fight against this, to fight with every weapon taken from him, forbidden to lie and yet brought to places where truth seemed fatal?" (*P*, 121). In the space of a few moments, Ransom has passed through the internal anguish of rebellion, doubt, and fear. Then, suddenly, "the spell was broken" (*P*, 121). Ransom rises to boldly utter his μή γένοιτο,[7] his "May it not be!" speech, delivering perhaps his best defense in these series of exchanges.

However, his best it is not quite enough. Ransom realizes that it cannot go on; that these rational arguments alone are insufficient weapons to fully counter the embodiment of evil present in the Un-man. Indeed, the way the Un-man so easily lays aside rational thought when Tinidril is not present presages Ransom's need to move beyond his intellectual resources if he is to preserve innocence.

C. S. Lewis had begun reading *The Revelations of Divine Love* by Julian of Norwich in 1940. In a March 21 letter to his brother, he talks about her concept of "the Grand Deed," some inconceivable act of God that will make all evil—including sin and pain—turn out right in the end. Lewis quotes the line where Christ tells Julian, again and again, "All shall be well, and all shall be well, and all manner of thing shall be well."[8] Then he writes,

> My mood changes about this. Sometimes it seems mere drivel. . . . But then other times it has the unanswerable, illogical convincingness of things heard in a dream and appeals to what is one of my deepest convictions, viz. that reality always escapes prediction by taking a line which was simply not in your thought at all. Imagine oneself as a flat earther questioning whether the earth was endless or not. If you were told "It is finite but never comes to an end", one wd. seem to be up against nonsense. Yet the escape (by being a sphere) is so easy—once you know it. At any rate, this book excites me. (*CL* II, 369–70)

In the plot of *Perelandra*, Ransom must take a line not in his thought at all. The spiritual battle must become incarnate. Ransom must put to good use the martial transformation he experienced on Malacandra. As he does, another transformation takes place. Ransom's quest to vanquish corporeal evil involves spiritual rather than intellectual growth. He must learn to conquer his fear, yield to the will of God, and be embraced by Paradise. Through identifying with the main character, the reader experiences vicariously a personal resolution of the problem of evil. With Ransom, emotional, volitional, and mystical resolutions are made, echoing various ways each Christian must ultimately resolve evils that defy rational explanations. This is imaginative theodicy at work.

Ransom's emotional resolution begins with his own horror at finding a froglike creature tortured. In Lewis's own life, when his wife was dying, he was on guard lest "my own present unhappiness harden my heart against the woes of others!"[9] Here Ransom's sympathy for the woes of another awakens his emotions: "It was like the first spasm of well-remembered pain warning a man who had thought he was cured that his family have deceived him and he is dying after all. It was like the first lie from the mouth of a friend on whose truth one was willing to stake a thousand pounds. It was irrevocable. . . . [Ransom] had passed into a state of emotion which he could neither control nor understand" (*P,* 109).

His human sympathies will become more complex during moments when he struggles to discern how much of Weston may still be alive in the Un-man. These passages are illuminated by the counsel Lewis gave to his brother when the latter speculated about demonic powers at work in certain Nazi: "Suppose your eyes were opened and you cd. see the Gestapo man visibly fiend-ridden—a twisted and stunted human form, covered with blood and filth, with a sort of cross between a mandrill and a giant centipede *fastened* unto it? Surely you, and the human remains, become almost allies against the horror which is tormenting you both, him directly and you through him?"[10] Yet the first example of human sympathy in *Perelandra* occurs much earlier, in the first chapter, when Ransom's friend braves an unseen barrage on the way to an English cottage. The author character Lewis might have turned back but for "some reluctance to let Ransom down" (*P,* 16).

Ransom's own emotional fears will have to be laid aside more than once as his struggle against evil becomes incarnate. Here, the struggles of one whose name is also "Ransom" are his emotional anchor and inspiration. Ransom's love for Christ and for the Green Lady—and for all of Perelandra for that matter—will compel him to conquer his fears. The task ahead will still be difficult. In chapter 11 we are told, "His fear, his shame, his love, all his arguments, were not altered in the least. The thing was neither more nor less dreadful than it had been before. The only difference was that he knew—almost as a historical proposition—that it was going to be done" (*P,* 149).

Ransom's volitional resolution occurs in this same chapter, when he realizes that the only decision ultimately before him is whether or not he himself will submit to the will of Maleldil. "His journey to Perelandra was not a moral exercise, not a sham fight. If the issue lay in Maleldil's hands, Ransom and the Lady *were* those hands. The fate of a world really depended on how they behaved in the next few hours. The thing was ir-reducibly naked" (*P,* 142). Here, again, is the "single naked choice" spoken of in *The Problem of Pain:* "of loving God more than the self or the self more than God" (*PP*, 18). He must do the right thing, not only because it is right but because it is God's will. On the garden planet of Venus, Ransom must find a way out of his own will. He must become more like Christ, the one who overcame fear in a different garden, yielded to the Father's will and was ministered to by an angel.[11] "In the end Ransom makes his choice: to attempt to destroy the Un-man physically."[12] Immediately after this submission, Ransom is granted deep rest.

Notice that in this volitional resolution Ransom has fully transitioned from passive observer (as he was in the first dialogue), to fully engaged advocate (in the latter dialogues), and on to active participant in body and soul. He is moving from the theoretical to the practical. The question is no longer, "Why is there evil?" but "What am I going to do about it?" If the reader has identified with the hero up to this point, then that same reader may begin to sense imaginatively the full weight of this decision. If so, he or she may also realize that each of us has choices to make, and that our choices matter. Now, Lewis was very clear that he did not begin to write *Perelandra* for this or any other didactic purpose. "I've never started from a message or a moral," he wrote. "You find out the moral by writing the story."[13] The starting point was creating a compelling world full of wonder. After that, "something has got to happen."[14] Yet compare the finished story here to what Lewis says in his 1941 lectures on Milton's *Paradise Lost:* "The cosmic story—the ultimate *plot* in which all other stories are episodes—is set before us. We are invited, for the time being, to look at it from outside. And that is not, in itself, a religious exercise. When we remember that we also have our places in this plot, that we also, at any given moment, are moving either towards the Messianic or towards the Satanic position, then we are entering the world of religion. But when we do that, our epic holiday is over: we rightly shut up our Milton."[15]

Lewis had explored this religious point that same year in his sermon, "The Weight of Glory." Our free will choices have eternal significance. Heaven and hell are in the balance. "All day long," says Lewis, "we are, in some degree, helping each other to one or other of these destinations."[16] Readers may grasp this and try to live more virtuously because of it, even if they cannot fully reconcile the presence of evil to God's goodness and power. If that is so, the volitional resolution has done its work. As Lewis had earlier advised, "a little courage helps more than much knowledge."

Ransom's mystical resolution will take him from the depths of the world to the heights of beatific glory. Here again Ransom is becoming more like Christ. The movement resembles Ephesians 4:9: "What does 'he ascended' mean except that he also descended to the lower, earthly regions." Other plot elements suggest the Protevanglion of Genesis 3:15: "He will crush your head, and you will strike his heel." Ransom notices that the Un-man, right before his destruction, "had hardly anything left that you could call a head" (*P,* 182). Later, he notices that his own most serious injury is "a wound in his heel" (*P,* 187).[17] The subterranean sojourn itself is a kind of death, burial, and resurrection.

The Great Dance at the close of Perelandra has been variously interpreted. Doris Meyers takes it as didactic: a "not entirely successful attempt" to teach that "nothing is random, everything is center."[18] But perhaps Lewis is attempting something grander here. Jeff McGinnis sees in it an image of heaven;[19] David Downing notes that the "exclamations heard during the Great Dance frequently echo declarations by mystical writers whom Lewis knew well";[20] and Sherry Dennis rightly notes that this is Ransom's "most intense experience of *sehnsucht.*"[21]

In the end, it may be best to view the Great Dance not in didactic terms but as an attempt to let the reader encounter a mystical experience. If so, then the scene is more than the sum of its parts. The reader participates vicariously in Ransom's mystical circle. Before the Dance, Ransom confesses that he is "full of doubts and ignorance" (*P,* 213). In the Dance itself, the "part of him which could reason and remember was dropped farther and farther behind" (*P,* 219). As Lewis said of his own conversion to theism, it is "total surrender, the absolute leap in the dark."[22] Not every question is answered, and yet Ransom discovers "a quietness, a privacy, and a freshness . . . the sense of stripping off encumbrances and awaking from trance, and coming to himself" (*P,* 219). The mystical resolution has done its work. From now on "the splendor, the love, and the strength" will be upon him (*P,* 222).

Note that this closing benediction for *Perelandra* is the same as the opening advice from the *Problem of Pain,* but in reverse order. Holding on to faith in God while encountering evil takes courage, human sympathy, and the least tincture of the love of God. Here, the blessings of God's continuing presence are splendor, love, and strength—the mystical, emotional, and volitional resolutions. The practical advice has become fleshed out in a fictional character so that it can be more accessible to a wider audience.

So what led Lewis to transition from an academic theodicy to this perhaps more practical imaginative theodicy? What happened between November 1939, when Lewis began *The Problem of Pain*, and November 1941, when Lewis begins to write *Perelandra?*[23] Well, what didn't happen? There was the Battle of Britain, Charles Williams's relocation to Oxford, refugee children at the Kilns, the beginning of correspondence with Sister Penelope, speaking tours to the Royal Air Force, the BBC broadcasts, *The Screwtape Letters*, and fan mail. Of all these significant developments, the most immediate catalysts appear to be Sister Penelope's influence and Lewis's work with the RAF.

Charles Gilmore says of the airmen who came to hear Lewis speak that "well over three-quarters of them were civilians in uniform, men and women now with time to think, knowing it to be important to get it right if they should survive the war. . . . [A]s a result of hearing Lewis there were handfuls of young people all gaining quite new concepts of how they fitted into the life that immediately lay before them."[24] Lewis, on a regular basis, was helping thoughtful airmen put enough pieces together to function well as airmen. On October 2, 1941, Lewis wrote to Mary Neylan, "I am hardly ever home for more than 3 consecutive nights and unable to arrange anything. I'm off to Aberystwyth to-morrow" (*CL* II, 492). (This is where the RAF No. 6 Initial Training Wing was based.[25])

In a letter to Sister Penelope dated October 9 of that year, he says of that visit, "So I lived for a weekend (at Aberystwyth) in one of those delightful *vernal* periods when doctrines that have hitherto been only buried seeds begin actually to come up—like snowdrops or crocuses. I won't deny they've met a touch of frost since (if only things would *last*, or rather if only we would!) but I'm still very much, and gladly in your debt" (*CL* II, 493). New surroundings, new acquaintances, new airman trying to get it right, new theological insights that Lewis is trying to get right: they come together in fresh ways at Aberystwyth. Lewis will increasingly find ways to disseminate these insights through new projects. A month later, he is writing *Perelandra.*

Though better known for his work as the twentieth century's great defender of a reasonable Christianity, Lewis was also able to employ other creative skills to promote his worldview. In *Perelandra,* the simple advice to confront evil with courage, human sympathy, and the least tincture of God's love is expanded and developed. As Ransom experiences volitional, emotional, and mystical resolutions to facing evil and holding on to faith, readers are able to try these practical approaches on for size. In this way, Lewis hoped to pass on practical counsel to his readers, so that "the splendor, the love, and the strength" would be upon them as well.

NOTES

1. C. S. Lewis, *CL* II (San Francisco, Calif.: HarperCollins, 2004), 121.

2. C. S. Lewis, *PP* (New York: Macmillan, 1948), 14.

3. This piece of advice on how to write well was offered by C. S. Lewis to the young Miss Joan Lancaster in a letter dated June 26, 1956. C. S. Lewis, *CL* III (San Francisco, Calif.: HarperCollins, 2007), 765.

4. C. S. Lewis, *P* (New York: Macmillan, 1965), 148.

5. C. S. Lewis, *MC* (New York: Macmillan, 1960), 52.

6. C. S. Lewis, "Evil and God," in his *GD* (Grand Rapids, Mich.: Eerdmans, 1970), 23.

7. One of the Apostle Paul's recurring lines in the book of Romans; see, for example, Rom. 3:4, 3:6, 3:31; 6:2, 6:15 (New International Version).

8. This is found in the Thirteen Revelation of Julian of Norwich's *The Revelations of Divine Love* (c. 1393) and is quoted by Lewis in a letter to his brother, W. H. Lewis, dated "Maundy Thursday, [19]40," in Lewis, *CL* II, 369.

9. C. S. Lewis to Mary Willis, Apr. 1, 1957, in Lewis, *CL* III, 823.

10. C. S. Lewis to W. H. Lewis, May 4, 1940, in Lewis, *CL* II, 409.

11. "'Father, if you are willing, take this cup from me; yet not my will, but yours be done.' An angel from heaven appeared to him and strengthened him" (Luke 22:42–43).

12. David C. Downing, *Planets in Peril: A Critical Study of C. S. Lewis's Ransom Trilogy* (Amherst, Mass.: Univ. of Massachusetts, 1992), 115.

13. C. S. Lewis, "The Establishment must Die and Rot . . . ," reprinted in *C. S. Lewis Remembered: Collected Reflections of Students, Friends and Colleagues*, ed. Harry Lee Poe and Rebecca Whitten Poe (Grand Rapids, Mich.: Zondervan, 2006), 237.

14. Ibid., 236.

15. C. S. Lewis, *PPL* (New York: Galaxy, 1961), 132.

16. C. S. Lewis, *WG* (Grand Rapids, Mich.: Eerdmans, 1965), 15.

17. Lewis later confesses to E. R. Eddison, "The bite on the heel is scriptural," in a letter dated April 29, 1943, in Lewis, *CL* II, 571.

18. Doris T. Myers, *C. S. Lewis in Context* (Kent, Ohio: Kent State Univ. Press, 1994), 71.

19. Jeff McGinnis, *Shadows and Chivalry: C. S. Lewis and George MacDonald on Suffering, Evil, and Goodness* (Milton Keynes: Paternoster Press, 2007), 278.

20. David C. Downing, *Into the Region of Awe: Mysticism in C. S. Lewis* (Downers Grove, Ill.: InterVarsity Press, 2005), 102.

21. Sherry K. Dennis, "Sehnsucht and the Island Motif in C. S. Lewis' *Out of the Silent Planet* and *Perelandra*" (M.A. diss., Florida Atlantic Univ., June 1978), 30.

22. C. S. Lewis, *SBJ* (New York: Harcourt, Brace & World, 1955), 228.

23. Lewis's first mention of writing *The Problem of Pain* occurs in a letter to his brother, W. H. Lewis, dated Nov. 11, 1939 (in Lewis, *CL* II, 289). The writing of a Ransom sequel is first mentioned by Lewis in a letter to Sister Penelope, dated Nov. 9, 1941 (in Lewis, *CL* II, 496).

24. Charles Gilmore, "To the RAF," in *Remembering C. S. Lewis: Recollections of Those Who Knew Him*, ed. James T. Como (San Francisco, Calif.: Ignatius, 2005), 311.

25. BBC, "RAF War Drawings Found at Hotel," BBC News, Apr. 12, 2007, http://news.bbc.co.uk/2/hi/uk_news/wales/mid_/6549573.stm.

Free to Fall

The Moral Ground of Events on Perelandra

MICHAEL TRAVERS

In his essay "On Science Fiction," C. S. Lewis explains that his Cosmic Trilogy—*Out of the Silent Planet, Perelandra,* and *That Hideous Strength*—should be understood as a subspecies of the genre of science fiction. The effect Lewis attempts in his science fiction is to create "another world, . . . actual additions to life" that "enlarge our conception of the range of possible experience"[1] both for the characters in the narratives and for the readers. In the case of *Perelandra,* the most startling "addition" is a sinless character, Tinidril, the unfallen "Eve" of the planet. Unlike the reader, she and her husband, Tor, have never disobeyed Maleldil (God's name in the narrative) and are therefore morally innocent. The resultant stark moral divide between Tinidril/Tor and the reader can easily create the impression that this "innocence" reduces Lewis's characters to the stereotypical and two-dimensional. In narrative terms, it raises the worry that the novel lacks any genuine moral tension to warrant the reader's consideration. This chapter attempts to meet these concerns by addressing the question of free will and moral responsibility on the parts of the novel's three major characters: Tinidril, Ransom, and Weston.

One of Lewis's basic assumptions in *Perelandra* is that unfallenness (innocence) and free will are by no means incompatible; on the contrary, free will makes a moral fall possible. The depiction of an unfallen character therefore does not abrogate the potential for moral conflict, but rather displays it in paradigmatic form. Conversely, it offers a new perspective on free will that questions the usual modern understanding of free will as existing only within a tendency toward evil.

In letter to Tony Pollock dated May 3, 1954, Lewis answers a question Pollock poses about the Fall. He writes, "*Perelandra* answers the view 'By a Fall, don't you really mean only the inevitable finiteness & incompletion of Man?' Answer: no, I don't, I believe it resulted from a free act of sin & could have been avoided. If God created any other rational animals in some other part of the universe, perhaps they did *not* fall. One may imagine. . . ."[2]

For Lewis, free will, or free choice, is a two-edged sword: a person may choose to do good, or he may choose to abuse his free will and do evil, or sin; both options are possible, and neither is determined ahead of time. The importance of Lewis's comment in the letter to Pollock is that it states clearly that a creature "innocent" of sin has a perfectly legitimate free choice to fall or not to fall. Tinidril's choices are legitimate in that, even in her sinless state, she is capable of choosing evil over good; her choices in the narrative, therefore, are morally significant.

LEWIS ON FREE WILL

Fortunately, C. S. Lewis's views on free will are well known. Around the time Lewis was writing *Perelandra* in the early 1940s, he addressed the problem of evil from the perspective of a freewill theodicy in a number of writings. In *Mere Theology*, Will Vaus argues that Lewis tends to emphasize free will over divine sovereignty in early writings such as *The Problem of Pain* and *Mere Christianity*, while in later works, including the majority of his fiction, he emphasizes God's sovereignty.[3] To be sure, Vaus recognizes that this dichotomy is an oversimplification, so he notes also that the first mention of grace in Lewis's writings is found in *Perelandra*, written contemporaneously with *The Problem of Pain* and the BBC "Radio Broadcast Talks," which were published later in book form as *Mere Christianity*.[4] Lewis is very much aware of the subtleties and nuances of the tension between free choice and divine sovereignty, yet he always emphasizes the responsibility that goes with free choice. So it is in *Perelandra*.

Lewis's argument begins with the idea that free will is grounded in an awareness of self as contra-distinguished from others—in effect, in self-consciousness. In *The Problem of Pain*, he writes, "The minimum condition of self-consciousness and freedom, then, would be that the creature should apprehend God and, therefore, itself as distinct from God."[5] To be free to choose, and thus to be responsible for choices, humans must be aware of themselves as individuals, apart from God and others and endowed with the power of self-determination. Lewis's position here is very close to the "libertarian freedom" view. Libertarian freedom is the idea that free agents perform actions for reasons, but these reasons "do not cause or determine them."[6] To be fair to Lewis, however, we need to acknowledge that his thinking on free will does not fall so neatly into the libertarian camp. In *The Great Divorce*, for instance, the character George MacDonald states that freedom is that gift "whereby ye most resemble your Maker."[7] Free choice is part of the *imago dei*, relating humans to God. The problem is that the same freedom that allows humans, as self-conscious beings, to obey God, also opens the door to the possibility of disobedience. In fact, in *Mere Christianity*, Lewis says as much: "And free will," he writes, "is what has made evil possible."[8] Again, in *The Problem of Pain*, Lewis states that the reason for problems in the universe is not God but simply "the abuse of [our] free will" (*PP,* 63). For Lewis, free will makes evil, as well as good, possible; in turn, the power to choose either evil or good renders every choice significant. "Free choice," he writes in *Mere Christianity*, is in fact "the only thing that morality is concerned with" (*MC,* 91).

TO TURN TO PERELANDRA . . .

If readers of *Perelandra* are to experience the moral conflict in the narrative, they must do so on the basis of the free will of the main characters. There are three main characters with markedly different moral conditions in the narrative: Ransom, Tinidril, and Weston. Tor, the King, does not personally enter the scene of conflict, appearing only at the end of the story; the moral conflict thus focuses on Tinidril's choices. Maleldil has imposed only one divine injunction on Tor and Tinidril, namely, that they not spend the night on the Fixed Land—a command that suggests that they are to depend moment-by-moment on Maleldil, rather than on the security of the Fixed Land. For Tinidril, the choice posed by her free will is whether or not she will continue to obey this command when tempted to resist it. Ransom introduces a different moral perspective into Tinidril's world, one with which she is not familiar at all: Like all humans from Thulcandra (Earth), he has sinned and disobeyed God and thereby has experienced evil personally. For Ransom, free will poses the choice of whether or not he is willing to surrender his wishes and obey Maleldil by defeating Weston before the latter can seduce Tinidril to evil. Weston himself presents yet a third moral perspective in the narrative: When he invites a dark power to possess him, he surrenders his free will altogether and becomes the "Unman," incapable of choosing moral good. For Weston, henceforth, there is no question of how he will use his free will. These three perspectives furnish the moral ground for the narrative.

RANSOM

Ransom is a fallen human being from Thulcandra, a planet under the influence of a fallen Oyarsa, whom Lewis calls the "Bent One" or "the Black Oyarsa" and who in Christian tradition is called Satan. During his time on Malacandra (an experience related in *Out of the Silent Planet*, the first novel in the science fiction trilogy), Ransom is brought face to face with the realization that his free will is inclined toward selfishness and self-centeredness. On Malacandra, he met three entirely different types of rational beings (or *hnau*, in the Old Solar tongue), all of whom coexist peacefully and do not desire to dominate one another. His meeting with the *sorn* Augray, who shows him Earth, is the point at which he most felt his distance from home and his isolation from other human beings (Weston and Devine notwithstanding) on Malacandra. "'That is my world,'" he says to Augray; "it was the bleakest moment in all his travels."[9] By this time in the narrative, Ransom has witnessed enough of the peacefulness of the *hnau* on Malacandra that he is aware of the sharp contrast they present with the evil of human beings like Weston and Devine—and himself; earlier, when he cradled Hyoi's dying body after he was shot, Ransom even admitted his culpability (*OSP*, 82). Now the sight of planet Earth, where so much evil exists, leaves him quite dispirited. Now, in his adventures on Perelandra (a journey chronicled in the novel of that name), Ransom is reminded of his sinfulness by his frequent meetings with Tinidril; still later, when Weston arrives on the planet, Ransom feels a great urgency to help Tinidril resist succumbing to the sin with which he is so familiar in his own life, and which he sees writ large in Weston's life. Ransom knows that he should help Tinidril resist Weston's temptations, so the issue is whether or not he will do what he ought to do for her. He is free to choose to help her or to stay out of the struggle altogether.

We can begin to understand Lewis's views of the natural inclination of a fallen human being's free will by observing his comments on the issue of conversion to Christianity. In "The Decline of Religion" (1946), Lewis writes, "Conversion requires an alteration of the will, and an alteration which, in the last resort, does not occur without the intervention of the supernatural."[10] Without divine intervention, sinful humans will not choose conversion. Fallen humans tend to be selfish and self-centered. This focus on self first is an expression of human nature in its postlapsarian, or fallen, condition. Lewis's statements about the quintessential sin of pride may provide a helpful gloss on the matter. In *Mere Christianity*, Lewis states, "Pride is the complete anti-God state of mind" (*MC*, 122). Human selfishness and pride—indeed, all expressions of human fallenness—put the creature in a contest of wills with the creator. For Lewis, goodness is achieved when a human will submits to the divine will, whereas sin is revealed when the human will chooses against the divine will. Free will for fallen humans, then, is inclined toward self and away from God; this is the state of Ransom's free will when he lands on Perelandra. This is the reader's moral condition as well.

Evidence of Ransom's sinful self-centeredness is written all over his lengthy struggle with his conscience in chapter eleven of *Perelandra*. Early in the chapter, he exercises his freedom by wishing that he did not have to be Maleldil's "instrument" to help Tinidril avoid a moral fall. Though this desire is entirely understandable, it is one indication of his selfish disobedience, for it puts him in a contest with Maleldil. By the end of the chapter, however, Ransom's attitude has shifted 180 degrees, as he realizes that predestination and free will are "apparently identical,"[11] and that submitting to Maleldil's will that he help Tinidril is not inconsistent with the exercise of his own free will. Lewis's statement about his own conversion is helpful here. In an interview by Sherwood Wirt, published as "Cross Examination," Lewis writes, "The most deeply compelled action is also the freest action. . . . I chose, yet it really did not seem possible to do the opposite."[12] Conversion involves the difficult decision to submit one's own will to another's will, namely, God's. In theological terms, Ransom has been "sanctified"—that is, set apart to a particular task—and thus he subordinates his will to the will of the one who commands the duty.

On the planet of Perelandra, Ransom's sanctification is caught up specifically in helping Tinidril to remain obedient to Maleldil and therefore to refrain from stepping outside his will in any way. Caught between the desire, on the one hand, to avoid fighting Weston physically, and the dawning realization, on the other, that "here in Perelandra the temptation would be stopped by Ransom, or it would not be stopped at all" (*P*, 124), Ransom chooses freely to fight Weston, no matter how odious the prospect is to him; it is for him a "frightful freedom" that he possesses (*P*, 126). We should not minimize how deeply Ransom feels this decision, for he knows he could well be killed in the combat (*P*, 128–29); even so, he chooses to submit to Maleldil's will and fight Weston. David Downing has it exactly right when he writes, "The great challenge of [Ransom's] second journey [i.e., the trip to Perelandra] is to overcome his self-will."[13] Ransom must choose to withdraw from his own wishes. However, even that is not enough; in addition to such a passive submission, he must willingly submit to another's desires, a feat of active obedience, not merely passive submission. As Downing puts it, Ransom must "overcome his habitual willfulness, to acknowledge this pressure as a Presence and to submit to a will greater than his own."[14] These struggles in chapter eleven, then, are the moral center of the novel for Ransom, for it is in this chapter that he overcomes the natural human inclination to selfishness and self-centeredness and turns instead to a willing and active obedience to a divine will that does not necessarily consider his comfort. Ransom's struggle ends in a signal victory, not only for him but for the whole planet of Perelandra as well. He fights Weston in a prolonged and particularly difficult physical contest, succumbs to physical and spiritual exhaustion after defeating Weston, and finally emerges a changed man—with a bleeding heel—to become the majestic and mystical character we meet in *That Hideous Strength*. By electing to submit to Maleldil's will that he fight Weston, abandoning his own desire not to fight, Ransom thereby chooses freely to obey.

WESTON

Weston presents an entirely different moral case for the reader than Ransom. Weston arrives on Perelandra in much the same moral condition as Ransom in the sense that he is free to do good or evil. His actions are not determined at this point in the narrative, though from the beginning he is certainly bent on tempting Tinidril to disobey Maleldil. In short order, however, he is overpowered by some form of demonic possession that ultimately abrogates his free will altogether; he becomes a body acting out another's will. At one point, he intentionally asks to be dominated by evil: "I am the universe. I, Weston, am your God and your Devil," he screams. "I call that Force into me completely." Immediately he is overcome with physical paroxysms and a demon possesses him—and this despite his horrifying and agonized plea that Ransom stop the demon in Christ's name (*P*, 82). To be sure, Weston came to Perelandra with evil in mind, but up to this point he could at least choose to repent. When he does not repent, however, he is sealed permanently in evil, becoming the moral opposite of Ransom's willing submission to Maleldil. While Ransom chooses to will Maleldil's will, Weston chooses the Oyarsa Thulcandra's will and therefore loses his free will by inviting evil into his being. From this point forward in the narrative, with few exceptions, Weston is driven by a force not his own, unable to exercise his free will again in defiance of the demon that possesses him. This loss of free will in Weston renders it impossible for readers to empathize with Weston morally from this time forward in the narrative, for they are still free to choose between good and evil.

As if to underscore Weston's loss of free will, the narrator begins to call Weston the "Un-man." The term *Un-man* indicates that Weston somehow has become less than human by his submission to a demon. He is certainly not less human physically, for he retains great, even superhuman, bodily strength, as his stamina and sheer physical force during the fight with Ransom attest. Rather, Weston is subhuman in a moral sense. Specifically, Weston is less than human because he no longer has free moral choice; morally, his actions now are determined. To borrow a term from *Mere Christianity*, he is an "automaton," devoid of free will and therefore inhuman (*MC*, 48). Significantly, Ransom unconsciously refers to the Un-man as "it" on numerous occasions.

Given many chances to repent, Weston chooses rather to persevere on his evil course and, in the end, is deprived of free will and therefore of the *imago dei* we all share. Weston's choices are exactly the opposite of Ransom's: Ransom submits his will to Maleldil and becomes truly free, while Weston submits his will to Thulcandra and loses his freedom altogether. The two men come to embody the divine and demonic aims for humankind outlined by the devil Screwtape in *The Screwtape Letters*; Screwtape tells his nephew Wormwood about God's love for humans and the devil's contrary desire to consume them. "To us," Screwtape writes, "a human is primarily food; our aim is the absorption of his will into ours, the increase of our own area of selfhood at its expense." The Un-man is Lewis's incarnation of a human consumed by the demons. On the opposite side of the equation, Screwtape goes on to lament the fact that God, whom he calls "the Enemy," wants to "fill the universe with a lot of loathsome little replicas of Himself—creatures whose life . . . will be qualitatively like His own . . . because their wills freely conform to His."[15] Such is Ransom. Weston's loss of free will presents a sharp contrast to Ransom's willing choice to submit to Maleldil, underscoring the great significance Lewis ascribes to free moral choice and the responsibility that accompanies it. In the end, readers cannot empathize with Weston, who has lost his free will, and are forced back to identify with Ransom, who retains his.

TINIDRIL

It is between these two choices that Tinidril's decision is suspended, and it is in Tinidril's free will that Lewis develops the moral tension of the novel. Will she, like Ransom, learn the lesson that obedience to the divine will produces true freedom or will she unwittingly choose the evil that leads to perpetual enslavement? Like Milton's Adam in *Paradise Lost,* Tinidril is "free to fall."[16] In her choices rests the fate of the planet Perelandra.

At the beginning of the narrative, when Ransom lands on Perelandra, Tor and Tinidril are sinless creatures, much like Adam and Eve prior to their Fall in the Garden of Eden, in that they have not disobeyed Maleldil. They are presented as mature adults in full control of their faculties, free to choose as they wish without any interference from Maleldil. Lewis provides the paradigm for Tor and Tinidril in a comment on John Milton's Adam and Eve in *Paradise Lost.* In *A Preface to Paradise Lost,* written in 1942, a year before *Perelandra,* Lewis states that Milton's Adam and Eve could not have aged prior to the Fall. "The whole point about Adam and Eve," Lewis writes, "is that, as they would never, but for sin, have been old, so they were never young, never immature or undeveloped. They were created full-grown and perfect."[17] It is logical for Lewis to associate sin with aging, for in our growing old we eventually die and in so doing fulfill the curse placed on Adam and Eve and all creation in the Genesis account.[18] In the Genesis narrative, disobedience is sin, and sin, in turn, leads to death. Aging is the natural result of the curse on sin. In the same vein, when Tinidril learns a new lesson from Ransom or Weston, she says she is "growing old." The imagery is coherent with the Genesis account, underscoring the possibility that Tinidril, like Eve before her, could indeed disobey. She is free to stand and free to fall. If she were not morally free, she, like Weston, would be an automaton—except that she would be determined to obey and carry out good actions, rather than disobey and perform evil actions.

From the beginning of the narrative, Tinidril risks falling into sin. The fact that she and Tor are prohibited from staying overnight on the Fixed Land suggests that they have the power and free choice to disobey the command; if this were not so, Maleldil would be a deceptive puppeteer, and that idea is simply inconsistent with Lewis's portrayal of God in the Ransom novels. Further, Tinidril is free to talk with Ransom and Weston, or not, as she wishes. She is under no obligation to carry on a dialogue with either man, nor is she compelled to ask questions of them. In the event, though, she asks a great many questions, so that it is she who prolongs many of the conversations. At the same time, it is significant that it is like- wise she who most often terminates the conversations and leaves—again underscoring her freedom. Her choices drive the action of much of the narrative before Ransom's physical fight with Weston. She is clearly aware of herself as contra-distinguished from Tor and God (*P,* 90), a condition of free will and moral responsibility in Lewis's view.[19] For instance, she plays a self-conscious role at one point, horrifying Ransom with the prospect that she might succumb to pride (*P,* 108–9). She demonstrates her self- consciousness even more vividly in the melodramatic scene when she dresses up in feathers at the Un-man's coaxing and looks at herself in the mirror. In fact, looking at herself in Weston's mirror shocks her: "Then she started back with a cry and covered her face," the narrator states (*P,* 116). Weston's scheme in this dress-up and mirror scene appears to be to get Tinidril to sin by admiring herself more than Maleldil. The horror of the incident is underscored for the reader by the fact that Tinidril and Weston are dressed in feathers, indicating that living birds had to die to provide their "costumes." The significance of the scene is further underscored by the presence of Ransom, who wishes Tinidril not to succumb to Weston's seductions because he understands the full implications of her possible fall. Of course, Tinidril does not understand the full import of the actions

Weston is urging her to, but, even so, she does exercise free choice in dressing this way at all. Tinidril's behavior is consistent with Lewis's comments on free will in *Mere Christianity*: "If a thing is free to be good it is also free to be bad." And again, "free will is what has made evil possible" (*MC*, 48). Tinidril is no automaton; she can disobey or not, as she wishes. If she were to choose evil, as Weston wishes, the inhabitants of Perelandra would experience death on a universal scale—not merely the isolated deaths performed by Weston—just as the inhabitants of Thulcandra do. The outcome of Tinidril's disobedience would be catastrophic for all. It is her choice; she is free to stand and free to fall.

The beautiful and elaborate Great Dance at the end of the novel similarly attests to Tinidril's free will. If it were not so, why should there be such universal celebration when Tinidril, unlike Adam and Eve, resists temptation? Lewis concludes the novel in the imagery of a Great Dance because dance is a form of expression that requires the willing cooperation of numerous separate and individual beings acting together to fulfill its choreography in harmonious unity. Each participant willingly submits to the will of the "Great Choreographer." The Great Dance represents the cosmic approval of Tinidril's free choice to submit to Maleldil's will. As the various creatures participate in the ceremony, one says, "All is righteousness and there is no equality. Not as when stones lie side by side, but as when stones support and supported in an arch, such is His order; rule and obedience, begetting and bearing. . . . Blessed be He!" (*P*, 184). Each dancer fulfills its own role, no two exactly alike, yet together creating a great harmony that blesses Maleldil; this is the outcome of Tinidril's obedience. Lewis's observations in *Mere Christianity* underscore how appropriate this understanding of the Great Dance is, for there he states that the only way people can fulfill the purpose for which they were created is to submit their wills to God's will—as each does when it takes its place in the ceremony. The Great Dance celebrates the fact that Tor and Tinidril have done just that. Tinidril's obedience to Maleldil in not staying overnight on the Fixed Land and her success in not succumbing to Weston's temptations influence the character of the entire planet.

CONCLUSION

This brief survey of the three primary characters in *Perelandra* indicates that C. S. Lewis maintains a moral tension throughout the novel. From our perspective as disobedient, and therefore fallen, human beings, it is difficult to imagine that there could be moral tension in a sinless being, but this is precisely what Lewis creates through Tinidril's choices, for they are infinitely important. Tinidril is vulnerable to a moral fall, it is true, yet she retains her sinless obedience throughout the novel, choosing to resist Weston's numerous temptations and to abide by Maleldil's prohibition against staying on the Fixed Land overnight. To underscore the tension, Lewis positions Tinidril between two opposite moral poles, represented by Ransom and Weston. Ransom is a fallen human from Earth whose moral inclinations are self-preservation and self-centeredness. Recognizing the significance of Tinidril's struggle, however, and prompted by the realization that he alone can help her remain obedient to Maleldil, Ransom chooses to submit obediently to the will of Maleldil. Ransom's physical fight with the Un-man is the ultimate expression of this obedience on his part. Weston presents exactly the opposite moral pole from Ransom. He intentionally invites evil into his being and, in so doing, loses all free will and becomes an automaton driven by a demon to tempt Tinidril to sin. Tinidril is suspended between these two moral poles. Given free will, as evidenced in her self-conscious understanding that she is separate from Tor, Ransom, Weston, and even Maleldil, Tinidril ultimately decides willingly to submit her will to Maleldil's and obey his commands. The result is what so many have called "Paradise Retained," and the evidence of her success in the moral struggle is written all over the last pages of the novel in the Great Dance. Here, in the climax of the novel, all individuals and all complexities are woven into one unified and coherent *univ*erse (properly so-called), each taking his or her place in the Great Dance. At the end of the Great Dance, Ransom realizes that "a simplicity beyond all comprehension, ancient and young as spring, illimitable, pellucid, drew him with cords of infinite desire into its own stillness," and he himself finds his part in that cosmic unity (*P,* 188). With that realization, Ransom is returned to Earth and Perelandra retains its paradisal nature—all the result of Tinidril's action of freely choosing to obey Maleldil.

Notes

1. C. S. Lewis, "On Science Fiction," in *"On Stories" and Other Essays on Literature*, ed. Walter Hooper (San Diego, Calif.: Harcourt Brace, and Co., 1982), 66.

2. C. S. Lewis, *CL* III (New York: HarperSanFrancisco, 2007), 466.

3. Will Vaus, *Mere Theology: A Guide to the Thought of C. S. Lewis* (Downers Grove, Ill.: InterVarsity Press, 2004), 49.

4. Ibid., 51.

5. C. S. Lewis, *PP* (New York: HarperCollins, 2001), 20.

6. Scott R. Burson and Jerry L. Walls, *C. S. Lewis and Francis Schaeffer: Lessons for a New Century from the Most Influential Apologists of our Time* (Downers Grove, Ill.: InterVarsity Press, 1998), 67.

7. C. S. Lewis, *TGD* (New York: HarperCollins, 2001), 142.

8. C. S. Lewis, *MC* (New York: HarperCollins, 2001), 48.

9. C. S. Lewis, *OSP* (New York: Scribner Classics, 1996), 96.

10. C. S. Lewis, "The Decline of Religion," in Lewis, *GD* (Grand Rapids, Mich.: Eerdmans, 1996), 221.

11. C. S. Lewis, *P* (New York: Scribner Classics, 1996), 127.

12. C. S. Lewis, "Cross Examination," in *Lewis, GD,* 261.

13. David Downing, *"Perelandra:* A Tale of Paradise Retained," in *C. S. Lewis: Life, Works, and Legacy,* ed. Bruce L. Edwards (Westport, Conn.: Praeger Perspectives, 2007), 2:37.

14. Ibid., 40.

15. C. S. Lewis, *SL* (New York: Simon and Schuster, 1996), 41.

16. John Milton, *Paradise Lost,* ed. Merritt Y. Hughes (1667; New York: Odyssey Press, 1957), 3.99.

17. C. S. Lewis, *PPL* (New York: Oxford Univ. Press, 1961), 116.

18. Gen. 3:17–19 (English Standard Version). One of the curses God pronounces when Adam and Eve first sin is death. The Apostle Paul makes the connection between sin and death explicit when he writes, "The wages of sin is death" (Rom. 6:23a). The aging process, which, of course, culminates in death, is the natural result of God's curse on human sin in the Garden of Eden.

19. Cf. Lewis, *CL* III, 466, cited earlier in note 2.

Contributors

NIKOLAY EPPLÉE is an associate fellow of the Institute of World Culture at Moscow State University. He is a translator and editor of Russian editions of C. S. Lewis's *The Allegory of Love, A Preface to* Paradise Lost, and *The Discarded Image* (*Novoe Literaturnoe Obozrenie*, 2013) and *The Latin Letters of C. S. Lewis and Don Jiovanni Calabria* (forthcoming in *Museum Graeco-Latinum*). He has published a number of articles on Lewis in Russian literary magazines (such as *Novoe Literaturnoe Obozrenie* [New literary observer] and *Voprosy Literatury* [Issues of literature]) and in *Sehnsucht.*

PAUL S. FIDDES is professor of systematic theology in the University of Oxford and director of research at Regent's Park College, Oxford. He is the author of numerous influential books, including *The Creative Suffering of God* (Clarendon Press, 1988), and *The Promised End: Eschatology in Theology and Literature* (Blackwell, 2000). He has most recently written on C. S. Lewis in *The Cambridge Companion to C. S. Lewis* (Cambridge Univ. Press, 2010).

MONIKA B. HILDER is associate professor of English at Trinity Western University, where she teaches children's and fantasy literature. She is author of *The Feminine Ethos in C. S. Lewis's* Chronicles of Narnia (Peter Lang, 2012), *The Gender Dance: Ironic Subversion in C. S. Lewis's Cosmic Trilogy* (2013), and *Surprised by the Feminine: A Rereading of C. S. Lewis and Gender* (in press). She is codirector of Inklings Institute of Canada.

WALTER HOOPER is one of the foremost experts on Lewis in the world. As Lewis's personal secretary, friend, literary executor, and editor, Walter has edited numerous works by the author, including *Poems* (Geoffrey Bles, 1964), the *Collected Letters* (HarperCollins, 2000–2006), and various essay collections. His own books include *Past Watchful Dragons* (Collier, 1979),

War in Deep Heaven: The Space Trilogy of C. S. Lewis (Macmillan, 1987), and *C. S. Lewis: A Companion and Guide* (Fount, 1996).

BRUCE R. JOHNSON is senior pastor of Scottsdale Presbyterian Church in Scottsdale, Arizona, President of the Arizona C. S. Lewis Society, and associate editor of *Sehnsucht: The C. S. Lewis Journal*. His articles on C. S. Lewis have appeared in *Sehnsucht* and *SEVEN: An Anglo-American Literary Review*.

MERIEL PATRICK is lecturer in theology and philosophy for Scholarship and Christianity in Oxford (SCIO), the visiting student program of Wycliffe Hall in the University of Oxford, for which she teaches courses on C. S. Lewis and a variety of other topics. Her work has appeared in *The Journal of Inklings Studies*.

SANFORD SCHWARTZ teaches literature at Pennsylvania State University, University Park. He is the author of various studies of modern literary, intellectual, and cultural history, including *C. S. Lewis on the Final Frontier: Science and the Supernatural in the Space Trilogy* (Oxford Univ. Press, 2009).

MICHAEL TRAVERS is professor of English and associate vice president of Institutional Effectiveness at Southeastern Baptist Theological Seminary in Wake Forest, North Carolina. He has published numerous articles and four books, including the edited *C. S. Lewis: Views from Wake Forest* (Zossima Press, 2008).

TAMI VAN OPSTAL is a homemaker and mother of two in Dallas, Texas.

MICHAEL WARD is senior research fellow at Blackfriars Hall in the University of Oxford and professor of apologetics at Houston Baptist University, Texas. A former warden of Lewis's home, The Kilns, he is the author of *Planet Narnia: The Seven Heavens in the Imagination of C. S. Lewis* (Oxford Univ. Press, 2007) and coeditor of *The Cambridge Companion to C. S. Lewis* (2010).

BRENDAN WOLFE is a past president and secretary of the Oxford C. S. Lewis Society and executive editor of the *Journal of Inklings Studies*. A

D.Phil. candidate in church history at the University of Oxford, he is a regular contributor to the *Bryn Mawr Classical Review* and is coeditor of *C. S. Lewis and the Church.*

JUDITH WOLFE is director of studies in theology at St. John's College in the University of Oxford. A past president of the Oxford C. S. Lewis Society, she is executive editor of *The Journal of Inklings Studies* and coeditor of several volumes on C. S. Lewis, including *C. S. Lewis and the Church* (T&T Clark, 2011). She has written both on C. S. Lewis (most recently for the *Cambridge Companion to C. S. Lewis*) and on philosophical theology, most recently under the titles *Heidegger's Secular Eschatology* (Oxford Univ. Press, 2013) and *Heidegger and Theology* (Continuum, 2013).

Index